Judith Gre

A Short History of Sierra Leone

(New Edition)

LONGMAN

Longman Group Limited
London

Associated companies, branches and representatives throughout the world

© Christopher Fyfe 1962, 1979

All rights reserved. No part of this publication may be reproduced, stored in a retrieval
system, or transmitted in any form or by any means, electronic, mechanical, photocopying,
recording, or otherwise, without the prior permission of the Copyright owner.

First published 1962
New edition 1979

ISBN 0 582 60358 7

Printed in Hong Kong by
Commonwealth Printing Press Co Ltd

Contents

List of Illustrations

Maps

Figures

Introduction

The first edition of this book appeared in 1962 and is now out of date. Since then much has changed. Sierra Leone has gone through its early years as an independent state. Also since 1962 the study of African history has developed immensely: it is significant that almost every work included in the list of 'Further Reading' (see page 158) was published since then. More important, historians have increasingly learnt to look at the African past as a subject for study in itself, not, as formerly, merely as an adjunct to the history of Europe.

I have therefore revised the book thoroughly, presenting some of it with a different emphasis, correcting errors, and adding new material, including chapters on Sierra Leone since independence. But adding has also obliged me to subtract. Otherwise it would have been too long. So some parts of the previous edition have been omitted, not because they are inaccurate, but to make it an appropriate length.

My understanding of Sierra Leone's history has been greatly deepened since 1962 through the work of other scholars — most notably Arthur Abraham, Adeleye Ijagbemi, Malcolm McCall, Martin Kaniki and James Lenga-Kroma — to whom I acknowledge my affectionate gratitude. I am also grateful to Talabi Lucan for some extremely helpful advice.

CHRISTOPHER FYFE
Centre of African Studies
University of Edinburgh

Acknowledgements

The publishers are grateful to the following for permission to reproduce photographs:

British Museum for figs 1, 2, 4 and 5; Church Missionary Society for figs 7, 8, 9, 10 and 14; Colonial Office Library for fig 6; Foreign and Commonwealth Office Library for figs 15, 17, 18, 19, 22 and 25; Fotomas Index for figs 12a, 12b, 12c and 12d; Hoa-Qui for fig 35; Alan Hutchison Library for fig 33; The Mansell Collection for figs 3, 13 and 26; Nigeria Magazine for fig 21; Radio Times Hulton Picture Library for figs 11, 16 and 27; Royal Commonwealth Society Library for figs 28, 31, 32 and 34; Sierra Leone High Commission for fig 36.

The cover photograph was kindly supplied by the British Museum. The publishers regret that they have been unable to trace the copyright owners of figs 23, 29 and 30 and would like to apologise for any infringement of copyright caused.

CHAPTER ONE
Early History

Wandering peoples

The first men and women evolved in north-eastern Africa. From there, their descendants moved gradually over the African continent and the rest of the world. Archaeologists have dug up their skeletons, and the tools they used, and from them have reconstructed the history of the remote past. It is clear from their findings that people have lived in coastal West Africa for many thousands of years.

These earliest inhabitants were hunter-gatherers, people who moved about from place to place seeking food. They hunted animals, and gathered fruit, vegetables and honey. Though their way of life was simple, they learned to understand the environment they lived in, and passed on their knowledge to their children. They organised themselves politically into small groups, moving about together for protection. In these ways they were able to maintain themselves from one generation to the next.

Settled peoples

Eventually these wandering peoples learnt to grow their own food, instead of looking for it. They began clearing patches of ground and planting crops. This gave them a permanent food supply in one place. They ceased to be wanderers, and became settled farming peoples.

Their whole way of life became different. They built houses near their farms and became villagers. Instead of hunting animals over long distances they bred their own animals to eat, and hunted only in the neighbourhood. The wandering peoples' homes had been wherever they happened to be. The settled peoples had fixed homes.

Their lives grew more enclosed. Men's work became more different from women's work — the women more tied to the home, once they lived in settled communities.

Each community, or group of communities, tended to be isolated from the neighbouring communities. Each had its own customs, often its own language. Hundreds of different languages are spoken in West Africa, indicating that people have lived there in isolation from one another over long periods of time, as it takes many generations for new languages to develop.

They did not necessarily stay for ever in the same place. If the soil became exhausted, or the population of the community grew too large, they might move to another place nearby. There were constant migrations, but on a small scale — little groups of people moving short distances to new homes.

The migrations seem usually to have been peaceful. No doubt there were sometimes wars between the different communities, but one community did not conquer another, and force its own ways and language on its defeated enemy. Each retained its own identity and co-existed with its neighbours. Today about twelve distinct languages are spoken in Sierra Leone, which shows that in the past one language group has never forced itself on the others by conquest.

The early states

The present Republic of Sierra Leone forms part of a coastal plain, the Upper Guinea Coast, stretching from Cape Verde to Cape Mount. Until the nineteenth century much of it was covered by thick forest. Behind the plain rise mountains. Many rivers flow from the mountains to the sea. They flow steeply down through rocks and rapids. They only become deep enough to be easily navigable by boats between about fifty to sixty kilometres from their mouths. People moving from inland to the sea had to travel on foot.

The present political boundary was only fixed in 1896. Until then people moved freely through the coastal country, making their own settlements, and fixing their own boundaries between themselves and their neighbours as was most convenient.

If we want to trace the migrations of the present peoples of Sierra Leone we can begin by looking at their languages. If several languages are similar to one another, we can infer that the peoples who speak them were once closely associated. Perhaps they moved originally from one common homeland, far away, to their present homes.

Some peoples have traditions recalling their migrations. Some Temne traditions say that they came originally from Futa Jalon, the mountainous country to the north, in what is today the Republic of Guinea. The Bulom have no such traditions. This suggests that they moved to the coast a very long time ago. The Limba, whose language is unrelated to those of their neighbours, also have no traditions of migration. They say they have always been in their present home.

Mende, Loko and Susu are Mande languages. The Mande speakers all once lived far inland. Some moved towards the coast by different routes. The Mende and Loko came to Sierra Leone from the south-east, the Susu from the north.

It has become usual in Sierra Leone to speak of these peoples as distinct 'tribes'. But in the past the distinctions between them were not as clear as is imagined today. The languages they spoke were not uniform. Temne spoken in one part of the country was different from Temne spoken in another. Even people who spoke the same language were divided from one another politically into small separate states, each with its own government. People felt a stronger loyalty to their own state than to any 'tribe'.

How they governed themselves

Most of these small states were governed by kings. Small though they were, their rulers were independent sovereigns. They did not take orders from any higher political authority. We should therefore describe them as kings and their states as kingdoms. Within each kingdom were smaller chiefdoms whose chiefs were under the authority of the king.

The inhabitants of each kingdom had to obey their king. But his power was not absolute. It was limited by a constitution. For instance, kings had councils which they had to consult on important matters, and be guided by their opinions. If the king wanted war and his council did not, there was no war.

There were also powerful secret societies which preserved law and order. The authority of the Poro Society stretched over many kingdoms. Poro was a society for men. Women had their own societies, like Bundu and Sande. Societies also served as schools where boys and girls spent a period of instruction before being initiated.

Laws and constitutions were not written down, as these people did not read or write. Instead they developed their memories, to retain and pass on information. Old people would recall what they had learnt and instruct the young. They, in turn, would eventually tell their children what they had learnt. In this way knowledge was transmitted orally from one generation to another. As old people were regarded as the most reliable sources of knowledge, they were highly respected.

Their activities were sustained by religious beliefs. The authority of the government was upheld by religion, as was their whole way of life. Farmers, hunters, fishermen, craftsmen and political leaders all performed special religious rituals to bring them success in their daily work. Their more important religious ceremonies were carried out with music and dancing of great complexity, for they were skilled musicians and dancers. When they fell ill, their doctors used religious rituals to treat them, as well as administering medicines. When they died there were elaborate funerals, particularly for kings. The dead were commemorated with ceremonies, for they did not believe that death divided them from their ancestors.

The economy

Rice was the principal food. The farmers cleared farms, planted crops, then next year cleared new farms. They learnt not to impoverish the soil by taking too many crops from the same place. They kept goats and poultry, and hunted wild animals. The seaside people caught fish. They used palm oil to cook their meals. Rice, vegetables, meat or fish, and palm oil provided them with a good nutritious diet.

Craftsmen carried on small industries. The seaside people manufactured salt, evaporating it from sea water. They cut down tall trees and hollowed them out to make canoes, sometimes as much as fifteen metres long, to be used for transporting goods, or in war. Weavers wove durable cotton cloths and fibre mats, decorating them with dyes made from vegetable juices. Potters manufactured pots out of clay. In the northern part of the country the rocks contain iron ore, which was extracted, smelted in furnaces, and worked into iron tools or weapons. Further north people kept cattle and made leather out of the hides.

Skilled carvers made sculptures out of wood, ivory or stone, to use in religious rituals. Most of their wooden statues and masks have now perished, eaten by termites. But many stone sculptures survive, particularly the small soapstone figures called *nomoli*, carved in a variety of styles.

Commodities were exchanged for one another. Salt from the seaside was traded for iron tools or leather goods made inland. Anyone with goods to trade brought them to the nearest suitable market. In this way regular trade networks grew up, linking the different parts of the country. Kings and chiefs benefited by the growth of trade and markets, as they could tax the traders.

Kings and chiefs built houses of mud brick, plastered white outside, furnished inside with finely woven mats. They sat on wooden stools

Fig 1 Nomoli

covered with leather. The poor had houses of wattle and mud.

Every man had as many wives as he could support. Women did much of the heavy work. Important people also had slaves who worked for them. Slaves had to obey their masters, but they formed part of the household, and were usually treated humanely.

Thus the economy was organised to provide food, shelter and clothing for everyone, and luxuries for those who ruled.

CHAPTER TWO

Import-export trade

Long-distance trade

By at least the eighth century AD a large-scale, long-distance trade was regularly carried on in West Africa. Gold mined in the West African forests was brought north to the cities on the southern edge of the Sahara, and transported there by camels across the desert to North Africa. African traders moved back and forth along well-established trade routes, bringing gold and other commodities in one direction and imported goods in the other.

A few long-distance traders visited the Upper Guinea Coast, bringing gold and other goods to exchange for salt, or for kola which grew in the forests. But the trade was small. Goods imported from far away were a rarity in the coastal country.

In the middle of the fifteenth century the pattern of trade changed unexpectedly. Portuguese sailors began voyaging down the West African coast, looking for a route to India. They made contact with the coastal peoples and began trading. In this way imported goods were made easily available to them through traders who came by sea.

The Portuguese gave names to the rivers and other natural features along the coast. They named the most conspicuous mountainous peninsula 'Serra Lyoa', ('Lion Mountain'), thinking its high mountains, rising suddenly from the surrounding plain, looked like lions. This name became changed over the centuries to 'Sierra Leone', and was eventually applied to the surrounding country.

At this time the peninsula and the coastline south of it was inhabited by Bulom (or Sherbro, as they are sometimes called). North of them, round the mouth of the Scarcies River and inland, were Temne. These were the peoples who first met the Europeans. Susu and Fula also came from inland to the coast to trade with them.

European trade goods were attractive. They included good quality metal ware — swords, cooking pots and other utensils. They also included a great variety of textiles, lengths of wool and cotton dyed in bright colours, and ready-made clothes as worn in Europe. Though these imported textiles were no more durable than locally woven cloths (indeed were often less durable), people liked them and wanted to wear them.

In order to secure these attractive articles the Bulom and Temne had to give something in exchange. The Portuguese wanted gold, but the

Fig 2 Ivory cup with lid, carved by Bulom craftsmen

supply from inland was small. They also wanted ivory. Tusks could be easily supplied, for there were many elephants in the forests. Bulom craftsmen also supplied carved ivory. The Portuguese were amazed by their skill, and commissioned them to make ornamental spoons and salt cellars.

Another commodity they wanted was bees wax. At this time people in Europe lighted their homes and churches with wax candles. High quality wax, made by African bees, was therefore in demand.

The slave trade

But the commodity the Portuguese and the other European traders who followed them chiefly wanted was slaves.

From the fifteenth century to the early twentieth century Europeans conquered empires all over the world. Till then they had seldom ventured beyond Europe and the shores of the Mediterranean Sea. A large part of the American continent came under their control. In the tropical areas they planted sugar and other plantation crops on a large scale and sold the produce in Europe. Until the nineteenth century when people began inventing machines to work for them, plantations had to be laboriously cultivated by hand. It was impossible to get free labourers to do such work, so the owners used slaves.

Much of America was sparsely populated. In the more populous parts the European invaders killed many people or infected them with unfamiliar diseases from which they died. As there were not enough slaves for all the plantations, the Europeans turned to West Africa, well populated with strong, healthy people, for a labour supply. It was in any case safer to import slaves from overseas, as they could not run away to their homelands.

Europeans had another reason for buying slaves in West Africa. From this time onwards the manufacturing industries of Europe were steadily expanding, producing more and more manufactured goods. These goods had to be sold, to provide profits for the manufacturers. West Africa was a large potential market, full of customers who were ready to exchange slaves for manufactures. In this way it was tied to the European export economy, receiving manufactured commodities and supplying human labour in return.

It must seem strange that African kings and chiefs should have been prepared to sell their own people to foreigners. They were condemning them, and their descendants, to a life of cruel misery. The slaves, once bought, were no longer treated like human beings. They were herded on board slave ships like animals, fastened with chains. About one in ten died on the voyage. Once they reached their destination they were sold again, to work on American and West Indian plantations for the rest of their lives. Their children too were slaves for life, and their children, generation after generation.

But at all times and in all countries there have been people ready to exploit others, and sacrifice them to their personal advantage. Had the African vendors not sold slaves, they could not have obtained the European goods they wanted. These goods came to include guns and gunpowder, recently invented in Europe, which greatly increased their military strength. Rather than do without these commodities, they sold their fellow men and women. But they got the worst of the bargain. Europeans were able to create wealth with the slaves they bought. The slave-trader sold them at a profit to a planter who used them to grow crops he himself could sell at a profit. But the African vendor only got in return for his slaves, goods that would one day wear out and have to be replaced — at the price of still more slaves.

How trade was organized

Heavy waves beat on the Atlantic coast of Sierra Leone, making it

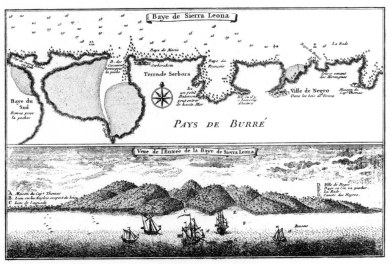

Fig 3 The Sierra Leone Watering-Place. Above is a map, below is the view from the sea (taken from a French book published in the eighteenth century)

impossible for sea-going ships to land. But the river-mouths provided safe anchorage. European ships' captains were particularly attracted to the Sierra Leone estuary, where, once past the treacherous rocks at the mouth, they could sail along a deep channel by the sandy bays below the mountains.

In the fourth bay was a stream of good, clear water (later called King Jimmy Brook). Sailing-ships had to be well supplied with water for their long, slow voyages; they also needed firewood to cook meals. So ships came regularly to the watering-place for water and wood. The king who controlled it was sure of getting regular opportunities to trade, which other kings inland would not have.

Other Europeans beside Portuguese came to the watering-place. At first some of them kidnapped slaves without paying for them. But that only involved them in wars, and spoilt trade. Normally trade was carried on by recognised rules.

The Europeans did not try to conquer the country, as they were doing in other parts of the world. The African rulers remained independent. In order to regulate trade they made laws which the Europeans had to obey. To prevent ships' captains stealing slaves, they made them send white sailors on shore as hostages as soon as they anchored. They levied customs duties — so much for water, so much for wood — which the Europeans had to pay.

Portuguese traders also ventured inland up the rivers. Some settled in the Loko kingdom of Mitombo. Their trading centre became known as Port Loko.

CHAPTER THREE
The Sierra Leone kingdoms in the sixteenth and seventeenth centuries

The Mani invade

Towards the middle of the sixteenth century an inland people, the Mani, invaded the coast. They conquered the country round Cape Mount and then set off in long war-canoes up the Atlantic coast. They were ferocious fighters (and were even said to be cannibals). They devastated Sherbro Island, which was then thickly populated, and went on to take the watering-place. Next they attacked Mitombo. No one seemed able to resist them.

Having conquered the coastal kings and taken their trading centre, they determined to strike inland and fight the Susu and Fula. But here they were at last defeated and pushed back to the coast again. From now on the Susu stopped coming to the watering-place to trade, and took their wares to the rivers to the north instead, particularly the Rio Nunez and Rio Pongas.

These wars did not stop trade — indeed trade increased, for the Portuguese bought those who had been taken prisoner. They followed the invading Mani up the coast, guided by the fires from the burning towns. One Bulom king gave himself up as a slave rather than fall into his enemies' hands.

Political changes after the invasion

The Mani, a small warlike group, were too few to people the lands they conquered. Their king went back to Cape Mount leaving sub-kings to rule the Bulom, Temne and Loko. These sub-kings and their successors gradually became independent kings, intermarried with their subjects and in time became identified with them.

So by about the middle of the seventeenth century the country was again composed of Bulom, Temne and Loko, though some of their kings and chiefs were Mani in origin.

But the boundaries of their countries were changed. The south shore of the peninsula and the watering-place were now controlled by Temne, not Bulom. Bulom still held the Bulom Shore, the north shore of the estuary, but were cut off from the main body of their people.

Temne also took Mitombo from the Loko. The Temne king who controlled the watering-place lived up the Sierra Leone River, and appointed a sub-chief to collect duties for him from the ships that put in for water.

After the sixteenth century Bulom sculptors seem to have stopped carving ivory for the Portuguese. Perhaps they were all killed by the Mani (or even taken away to work in Portugal). These beautiful objects were never made again in Sierra Leone.

Christian missionaries

In 1605 an elderly Portuguese priest, Father Barreira, a member of a Roman Catholic missionary organization, the Jesuit Order, came to preach the Christian religion in Sierra Leone. He baptized several kings and chiefs, including the ruler of the watering-place, who took the name Dom Philip de Leon.

A Susu king living up the Scarcies River invited him to his country. Old though he was, he set out by canoe. A storm suddenly broke, and he was nearly drowned; then he had to land and walk for two days through thick bush to reach the king's town. The king welcomed him in a friendly manner. But after he had been there a few days a Muslim arrived from the north and advised the king not to be baptized. So the king kept his own religion and was converted neither to Christianity nor Islam, and the old missionary returned disappointed.

In succeeding decades other Roman Catholic missionaries came to Sierra Leone. But they made few converts; most people preferred their own religion. By the end of the century regular mission work was given up, though passing priests paid occasional visits.

English traders

From the beginning of the seventeenth century English traders began coming regularly to Sierra Leone. As well as slaves and ivory they bought camwood, a hard timber used for making red dye. There were then many camwood trees near the coast, but eventually they were all cut down. Then in the nineteenth century chemical dyes were invented and camwood ceased to be valuable.

English traders settled in the Sierra Leone estuary on an island which they called Bence Island (today called Bunce Island), and on York Island, off the north-east corner of Sherbro Island. They did not own these trading posts. They paid rent to a Temne king for Bunce Island and to a Bulom king for York Island. They also had to pay for the right to trade, and various other duties. If trading posts were opened in the surrounding country they had to make similar payments to the kings and chiefs who ruled there.

Bunce Island and York Island were strongly fortified with thick stone walls. If they were attacked, the defenders sheltered behind them and shot out heavy iron balls from iron cannon. But as they were seldom attacked, the garrisons lived easy, sleepy lives and lost all interest in fighting. When an enemy came they were usually unprepared, and in any case did not feel like fighting, so the forts were easily captured.

There were many Afro-Portuguese living in the neighbourhood, descendants of Portuguese traders and their African wives, who would act as agents for Bunce Island. Some grew rich and powerful.

In 1726 a new Governor came out from England to Bunce Island. He was jealous of the Afro-Portuguese, and wrote to his employers in England that he was going to turn them all out of the river. But the most powerful among them, Lopez, joined with the king on the Bulom Shore and attacked Bunce Island one night. The Governor was taken unawares in bed. He ran out in the dark, waving his sword, but then decided it would be better to take refuge on the nearest ship. So he abandoned the island, and the fort was destroyed.

Mende and Vai migrations

The Mende peoples lived inland, but were gradually moving towards the coast. Unlike the Mani, they migrated slowly and peacefully. Small communities would move short distances to new homes, clear the land there and farm. They also traded. By the end of the eighteenth century they were going regularly back and forth to the sea coast, trading woven country cloths for salt.

The Vai people lived round the mouth of the Moa, or Gallinas, estuary. They had originally migrated there from inland. Some say they are the descendants of the Mani. It is also said that while they were travelling on their journey coastwards, some of them grew tired and decided to settle down in the mountains. They are known as Kono.

CHAPTER FOUR
Islam

Islam in West Africa

Islam was introduced into North Africa by Arabs in the seventh century. During successive centuries, long-distance traders, Arab and African, brought it across the Sahara to West Africa. The great commercial cities of inland West Africa became Muslim centres, particularly Timbuktu where famous Muslim scholars congregated and taught.

Long-distance traders usually adopted Islam. It was an international religion which suited their way of life. When a Muslim trader from one trading centre arrived in another, he would be welcomed there by his fellow Muslims, who looked after him.

But the country people, who formed the vast majority of the population, kept their own religions. They had no reason to adopt Islam. The Muslims were therefore only a small minority in West Africa. But they were influential and powerful.

The Holy War of Futa Jalon

The Fula people were dispersed over West Africa. Many of them preferred keeping cattle to farming. Instead of settling permanently in one place, they would move about seeking new pastures for their cattle. Some became traders and adopted Islam.

During the seventeenth century many Fula, some of them Muslim, some non-Muslim, moved into Futa Jalon under the rule of Yalunka and Susu kings. There were also some communities of Muslim Mandinka in Futa Jalon, traders and scholars.

Both groups, the Muslims (Fula and Mandinka) and the Fula herdsmen, were dissatisfied. The Muslims disliked being under the rule of non-Muslims. The Fula objected to paying taxes to Yalunka governments. Early in the eighteenth century they resolved to go to war. The war was partly a holy war (in Arabic, *jihad*) to spread the Muslim religion, and partly a political war to bring Futa Jalon under Fula rule.

14

The war started in about 1725. There were two famous leaders — Karamoko Alfa, a pious scholar, and Ibrahima Suri, a great general. At first Karamoko Alfa led the war, without much success. Then Ibrahima Suri took command and was ultimately victorious. By the end of the eighteenth century he had made Futa Jalon a Muslim Fula state.

This successful *jihad* inspired Muslims in other parts of West Africa to start similar wars against their governments — most notably the *jihad* of Usuman dan Fodio in Hausaland.

The effects of the war on Sierra Leone

Many Susu refused to change their religion and were driven out of Futa Jalon. Others were converted, but left rather than submit to Fula leaders. Some moved towards the coast to dominate the country north of the Scarcies. Some settled among the Limba. At first they would settle peaceably; then they would seize power. Many Limba moved away to the mountains, where they built high inaccessible towns to be safe from invaders.

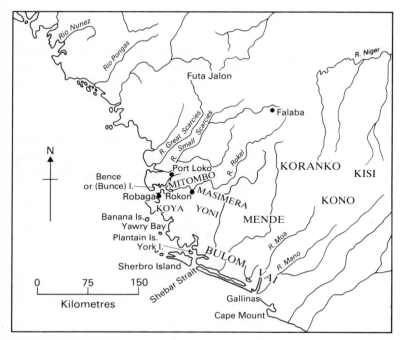

Map 1 The Eighteenth Century

One Susu group went to Port Loko, where the Temne chiefs let them build their own town, Sendugu. Gradually their power increased. Eventually they put down the chiefs and took over the government of Port Loko.

The Sulima Yalunka in Futa Jalon at first accepted Islam and joined the Fula in the war. But when the Fula grew powerful they became afraid of them, gave up Islam and turned against their allies. There was a hard struggle in which the Fula were finally victorious. The Yalunka were driven out of Futa Jalon and in 1768 founded a strong fortress-town in the mountains at Falaba. Some moved further into the mountains and became chiefs among the Koranko and Kisi.

Though these immigrants from the north came as invaders and rulers, the Sierra Leone peoples did not resist them much. Some welcomed them. Some Loko invited a Mandinka to help them in war; he became their king and his descendants ruled alternately with a Loko king. A Fula became chief in the Yoni country south of the Rokel. Non-Limba chiefs ruled the Limba. So over a wide area it became usual for peoples to have rulers of alien origin.

The spread of Islam

Muslim influence spread out from Futa Jalon. As trade with Europeans expanded, more Muslim traders visited the coast. They were welcome visitors, for, as well as bringing trade, they sold charms against sickness, and claimed to be able to tell the future. As they could usually read and write Arabic, kings and chiefs found them useful, and employed them as secretaries.

But they made few converts to Islam. Sometimes a ruler might become a Muslim, but his subjects usually kept their own religion which suited their particular way of life. Thus Islam was spread widely in Sierra Leone but not yet deeply.

CHAPTER FIVE

Trade and politics in the eighteenth century

Landlords and strangers

During the eighteenth century more of the American continent was cultivated and the demand for African slaves rose steadily. The main centres of the slave trade were to the south — Angola, the Bight of Benin (today the coast of Nigeria) and the Gold Coast (today Ghana). But about three thousand slaves were sold every year from the area round Sierra Leone.

After Lopez destroyed the Bunce Island fort, it was rebuilt. Many of the old walls are still standing today. But most of the trade passed through the hands of small European traders who settled singly or in groups by river-mouths or on islands along the coast.

A trader would pick on a suitable town, usually near the mouth of a river or on an island, so that he could sell his slaves to sea-going ships. He would then ask the chief's permission to settle there. Usually the chief was pleased: if he had a European in his town he was sure of getting trade. The trader would give him a present and pay him a regular rent. Some chiefs would take a percentage of the price of each slave. If the chief were an inferior ruler, his king would also exact payments from the trader.

When the agreement was made, the chief became the trader's 'landlord', the trader became the chief's 'stranger'. The landlord was responsible for his stranger's safety and looked after him. If the stranger quarrelled with another chief, his landlord settled the dispute. If the stranger committed a crime, the landlord took the blame. This system might give the landlord trouble but it prevented the stranger from interfering in politics. If several chiefs met to discuss some important matter, even if it were a matter that concerned European trade, Europeans were not admitted. They were strangers and could have nothing to say. Thus the chiefs preserved their political independence.

The landlord did not let his stranger travel up-country. He was afraid the stranger might find a new landlord and never come back. Instead of going to look for trade he had to stay in his landlord's town with his stock of goods, waiting for trade to come to him.

If none came, he gave goods to people in the town who took them up-country and brought back slaves, ivory or camwood. If these agents failed to return, the trader complained to his landlord. As the landlord was responsible for collecting his stranger's debts, he paid what the agent owed and then seized the agent's wife or children and sold them as slaves. This meant that the trader could safely give credit to agents, knowing that he would not lose by it.

How slaves were obtained

Most of the slaves sold on the coast were prisoners captured in war. Many taken in the wars in and around Futa Jalon were sold. The Susu and Yalunka sold their Limba and Kisi captives, who were brought from inland to the river-mouths where the European traders were waiting.

But on the coast, when there was peace, no one was sold without being first accused of an offence. Thieves were sold, or anyone who took another man's wife, but the most usual accusation was witchcraft.

Everyone then believed that no one becomes ill or dies without being bewitched, so if an important man died, someone was accused of bewitching him. The accused was not tried by asking questions, or by trying to find out evidence against him. He was given 'red water' — a drink made of herbs with pieces of kola in it — and then carefully watched. If within a certain time he brought up the drink and all the kola, he was innocent, and his accuser had to pay him a slave. If he did not, he was sold.

This custom enabled an unscrupulous chief to sell people whenever he wanted. If a trader said twenty slaves were urgently needed to make up a shipload, the chief would say he felt ill. He would accuse twenty people of bewitching him, arrange the trial so that they were found guilty, and sell them.

European slave-traders

European traders lived quiet, easy lives. Their landlords protected them, gave them wives (in Europe they were only allowed one) and brought them trade. But men who live by buying and selling others, and treating people as merchandise, grow cruel and brutal. They lose respect for humankind. No one could trust these traders who always cheated and lied to get a good bargain. Once a European trader in the Sherbro country accused an agent of cheating him. 'What!' the agent replied, 'do you think I am a white man?'

Yet these brutal demoralized men were welcomed for the goods they brought. During the eighteenth century new methods of weaving and spinning textiles were invented in Europe. More and better kinds of cloth were imported into Africa. People developed a taste for American tobacco (grown in America by African slaves) and for European drinks like brandy and rum. But they could not get these things without exchanging slaves for them.

Chiefs and the slave trade

Chiefs ordered fine clothes from England — embroidered coats, silk breeches and stockings, shoes with silver buckles. Such were the fashion in those days. Seeing the traders using chairs and tables they did the same. Some sent their children to school in England. Friendly slave-traders would take the children and bring them back when their schooling was finished. They did not receive any higher education, but they learnt to read and write, and hoped with their knowledge to be able to outsmart European traders.

Yet the chiefs did not really benefit. The slave trade created wealth for Europeans but not for them (see pages 8–9). The goods they bought wore out, or were smoked or drunk; and had to be replaced. Though they relied on their people to support them, their people also looked to them for support. If they had goods and their people asked for a share, they could not refuse. So they could not accumulate wealth.

A new kind of chief

Some Europeans married into chiefs' families and their children sometimes became important men. In Vai country the Rogers family, descended from a European and a Massaquoi (the ruling family among the Vai), grew almost as powerful as their royal relatives.

Henry Tucker was the biggest trader in the Sherbro country in the middle of the eighteenth century. He was of mixed descent, part Bulom, part European, and ruled at Bahol at the Shebar Straits. He had visited Europe and he lived in grand style, eating his dinner off silver plates. Such a man was stronger than the neighbouring kings, for his power was not limited, as theirs was, by tradition and custom.

In 1684 Thomas Corker, a young Englishman from London, came to the Sherbro and eventually rose to be Chief Agent at York Island. He married a lady of the Ya Kumba family which ruled the shores of Yawry Bay between the Sierra Leone peninsula and the Sherbro estuary. Their descendants kept the paternal surname Corker (which they spelt Caulker) but established their claim to rule the maternal chiefdom, which they extended to include the Plantain and Banana Islands. These islands were busy slave-trading centres, regularly visited by ships from Europe. The Caulkers grew rich and powerful.

A daughter of the Caulker family married William Cleveland, an English trader who settled on the Banana Islands. Their son James turned against his relatives the Caulkers. He had been sent to school in England to learn European ways, and on his return he joined Poro to learn African ways. The Caulkers were not then members, so he could act secretly against them. In 1785 he sent an army to the Plantain Islands, surprised Chief Charles Caulker, and cut off his head. This made him the most powerful ruler in the area.

When he died his nephew William, who was lazy and easy-going, succeeded him. For several years the Caulkers were too busy disputing among themselves to avenge Charles's death. Then Chief Stephen Caulker attacked William. He fled, and Stephen got back the Banana Islands.

William found allies in the Sherbro country, and for many years Clevelands and Caulkers went on fighting. Such wars were profitable to the European slave-traders, because when either side won a victory there were captives to buy. But there was also the risk that their stores might be destroyed in the fighting.

Stephen Caulker died in 1810, and by custom his brother Thomas was his successor. But his son George had been educated in England and had learnt there that under English law the eldest son, not the brother, succeeds. Rather than go to war with him, Thomas agreed to divide the chiefdom. He took the mainland and the Banana Islands, while George took the Plantain Islands.

So, although the slave-traders were kept from interfering in political affairs, the slave trade affected the government of the country indirectly. It enabled men of Eurafrican descent to use their wealth, gained by trade, to get political power.

Ngombu Smart

One day the son of a Loko chief killed a man, and as punishment was sold as a slave at Bunce Island. He was so clever that the slave-traders did not ship him across the Atlantic, but employed him as an agent, giving him the name 'Smart' because he was a smart man. They sent him up the Rokel to buy slaves. He bought chiefly his own Loko country-men, but instead of sending them to Bunce Island he trained them as a private army of his own.

When his neighbours went to war they called on him for help. In return for assistance Bai Simera, an important Temne king, let Smart and his Loko followers settle at Rokon on the Rokel. There he built a large town. He joined the Wonde Society and took the name Ngombu ('fire'). A successful trader as well as fighter, he became one of the most important men in the country.

CHAPTER SIX

The Province of Freedom and the Anti-Slave Trade Movement

Africans in London

Many Africans lived in England in the eighteenth century. Most had been brought there from slavery in America or the West Indies. It was uncertain whether under English law they could still be treated as slaves. In 1772 Granville Sharp, an Englishmen with a horror of slavery and the slave trade, arranged for an African, James Somerset, to be brought before the lawcourts to test whether or not slavery was legal in England. The judge would not give a clear answer, but he declared that Somerset could not be sent back to slavery in the West Indies. This decision gave former slaves some security once they arrived in England.

In 1775 thirteen of the British colonies in North America revolted against the Government. They fought until 1783 when the British gave in, and the colonies became an independent country, the United States of America. During the war the British offered slaves freedom if they left their American masters. Many ran away and joined the British army and navy. After the war some of them came to London, where they were free. But, though free, they were unemployed and had to beg in the streets.

Granville Sharp became their champion. He persuaded the British Government to take charge of them and send them to start a new home of their own in Africa. Although many of them had been born in America and had never seen Africa, they were nevertheless excited by hopes of returning to their ancestral home. The Government paid to send them there and gave them supplies. But their settlement was a self-governing state, named by Sharp the Province of Freedom.

The Province of Freedom

The settlers left England for Sierra Leone in April 1787. As most had no wives they brought seventy European women with them. Altogether they numbered four hundred and eleven.

They anchored at the watering-place in the Sierra Leone River, which was part of the Tèmne kingdom of Koya. The kingdom was ruled by a regent, Naimbana, who lived up the river at Robana and Robaga. A sub-chief, King Tom, governed the watering-place for him; his town was on the piece of land that still bears his name.

King Tom was given £59 worth of goods. In return he put his mark to a treaty giving up all claim to the shore sixteen kilometres east of the watering-place and thirty-two kilometres inland.

The settlers encamped on a hill near the watering-place (where State House now stands). They called their town Granville Town

Fig 4 The Province of Freedom (a view taken from near the present State House)

after Granville Sharp and elected one of themselves, Richard Weaver, as Governor.

Soon after they landed the rains began. They had only tents and rough huts to live in and were unused to such conditions. Day after day the rain beat down their shelter. Many fell ill and died; others went away to live with nearby slave-traders.

When Sharp heard of their plight, he sent them more supplies. The ship's captain who took them persuaded Naimbana, who had not agreed to the first treaty, to make a new one. For £85 worth of goods (chiefly clothes, food and drink) he gave up claim to the shore, as King Tom had done.

After King Tom died, his successor, King Jimmy, had many disputes with the settlers and with the slave-traders at Bunce Island. In 1789 the Bunce Island agent complained about him to the captain of a passing British naval ship, and the captain burnt one of his towns. In this dispute

23

the settlers sided with the captain. So when the naval ship had gone, King Jimmy retaliated on them, ordered them out of Granville Town and burnt it down in revenge for the burning of his own town. The settlers scattered over the country, and the Province of Freedom came to an end.

The Anti-Slave Trade Movement

The slave trade brought many Europeans big profits. Those who bought and sold slaves, those who made the goods they were bought with, and those who owned the ships they were carried in, all made money by it. But there were also some who, like Granville Sharp, thought it wicked and wanted it stopped. During the eighteenth century more and more people began speaking and writing against it.

John Newton was one of them. As a young man he worked in the Sherbro country buying and selling slaves, then became a ship's captain taking slaves across the Atlantic. One day he was nearly shipwrecked. His narrow escape made him think of religion. Gradually he realized that the work he was doing was wicked and unchristian. He gave it up, returned to England, became a clergymen, and preached against the slave trade. He also wrote many hymns which are still sung in Christian churches.

Two Africans living in England added their voices to the growing outcry — Ottobah Cugoano, a Fanti, and Olaudah Equiano, an Ibo. They wrote accounts of their lives, which were published as books, telling how they had been sold as children in Africa, then carried across the Atlantic, and finally had made their way to freedom in England. They appealed to the British Government to stop the cruel slave trade. They also pointed out that British traders would in the long run make more money if they treated Africans as customers not as merchandise — that is, if instead of selling them, they sold them goods.

In 1787 Thomas Clarkson, a young man who had determined to devote his life to abolishing the slave trade, formed a committee to work against it. Granville Sharp joined. They hoped to persuade the British Parliament to pass an act making it illegal. Their spokesman in Parliament was William Wilberforce, a rich young man who, like Clarkson, devoted himself unsparingly to the cause.

Clarkson and his friends travelled all over England making speeches against the slave trade. The main slave-trading centres were the cities of Liverpool and Bristol. There few listened. But in other cities where no one was making money out of slaves, thousands signed Clarkson's

24

petitions. At this time many new factories were being opened in England, and the owners were looking for more customers for their goods. They were impressed by the argument that they might find customers in Africa if the slave trade were abolished.

But the Members of Parliament were afraid of abolishing a trade that brought such big profits. Year after year Wilberforce made speeches against it, but they would not pass his act.

CHAPTER SEVEN
The Sierra Leone Company

The Foundation of the Company

A company was founded in London in 1791, the Sierra Leone Company, to take over the land Naimbana had granted. Sharp, Wilberforce and Clarkson were among the directors. It was a trading company but it did more than trade. Its directors wanted Sierra Leone to become a centre to provide Africa with the good things Europe could offer, instead of the evil slave trade.

They prohibited slave-trading within their territory, hoping to encourage Africans to grow produce for sale instead of selling slaves. They proposed to start schools where Africans could send their children, and to employ missionaries to teach them the Christian religion. They promised that any African who came to live under their rule would be treated as equal with the Europeans there.

Under the Company's rule the settlement was not self-governing like the Province of Freedom. The directors, in London, made laws and appointed European officials. The chairman of the directors was a London banker, Henry Thornton, a friend of Wilberforce. Granville Town was rebuilt and renamed Freetown.

The Nova Scotian settlers

After the American War of Independence many slaves from the American plantations, freed by the British army, were taken to the British colony of Nova Scotia, north of the United States. There they were free, and the government promised them land to farm. But years passed and many never got their farms. They were settled in remote areas of thick forest. In winter it was bitterly cold.

Among them was Thomas Peters. He had escaped from his master during the war and served as a sergeant in the British army. He waited six years and never got his land. Then he decided to go to England and complain to the Government. This was a brave decision. He was poor

26

and had no influential friends to help him; England was far off and unknown. Nevertheless he managed to reach London, and got in touch with the directors of the Sierra Leone Company, who offered his people land in Sierra Leone.

John Clarkson, Thomas's brother, a naval officer, went to Nova Scotia to bring the emigrants across the Atlantic. They were delighted at the chance of getting land in a home of their own in Africa where they or their ancestors had originally come from. Eleven hundred and ninety of them sailed from Nova Scotia in January 1792.

The Company was lucky to get these Nova Scotians. They were good settlers, self-reliant and anxious to farm. They were Christians — Methodist, Baptist and Countess of Huntingdon's Connexion — with their own preachers. Some were well educated enough to hold minor official posts. They were familiar with English law, so the Company could set up law courts on the English model and let them sit on juries.

Clarkson was put in charge. He had many difficulties, for his European subordinates were jealous of him, and so was Thomas Peters, who wanted to be Governor himself. After a short while the rains started. Like the first settlers they were unprepared and many fell ill. Nearly half the European officials died, and about a tenth of the Nova Scotians. Among them was Thomas Peters, disappointed of his hopes of being Governor.

Though Thomas Peters died disappointed, he was the real founder of the Sierra Leone Colony. Had he not courageously ventured to London, the Nova Scotians would never have settled in Sierra Leone, and without them the Company could never have kept it going.

Allotting the land

As the Nova Scotians had been cheated of land in Nova Scotia, they were determined to get it in Sierra Leone. After the rains, farms were surveyed east of Freetown. Naimbana and his people were alarmed, not having realized the Company was going to extend so far. Clarkson promised not to disturb their towns.

West of the watering-place the land belonged to King Jimmy, so the Nova Scotians had to be given farms inland in the mountains rising behind Freetown, where much of the ground was steep and rocky. There was no room to give them the large farms the Company had promised them, and Clarkson had to persuade them to take small farms instead. As they loved and trusted him, they agreed.

Clarkson left in December 1792. In succeeding years new governors were sent from England. The most famous was Zachary Macaulay. As a young man he had gone from Scotland to work in the West Indies. There he was so disgusted by the cruel way the slaves were treated that he left his job and determined to do all he could to fight slavery. Eventually he lived to see it abolished in the British colonies, largely through his own efforts.

The French plunder Freetown

From 1793 until 1815, with only one short interval, there was war in Europe between Britain and France. In wartime trade is dislocated and prices usually rise.

The Sierra Leone Company had to pay more for goods and raised prices in the Freetown store where the Nova Scotians did their shopping. When they complained, the European officials answered with lectures and rebukes instead of explaining patiently and kindly, as Clarkson had. Gradually the Nova Scotians lost confidence in the Company, which seemed to be neglecting their interests and had broken its promise to give them big farms.

No one supposed the French would attack Freetown, so there were no proper defences. But in September 1794 a French naval squadron sailed into the harbour and bombarded it. Then the sailors landed and went from house to house, stealing or destroying anything of value and shooting the livestock. The inhabitants took to the bush, leaving

Fig 5 Freetown in 1798, rebuilt after the French attack

their homes to be ransacked. The French stayed there over a fortnight, and before leaving burnt down all the Company's buildings.

As well as destroying the Company's property they captured several of its ships with large cargoes on board. These heavy war losses made it impossible for the Company ever to make any profit.

Freetown was rebuilt after the French had gone: the street layout still remains in central Freetown today. Macaulay built a governor's house on Thornton Hill (called after Henry Thornton). Some of the Nova Scotian farmers discovered coffee bushes and made coffee plantations. Others built boats, and went up the rivers to trade goods with the Temne and Bulom for rice.

The Maroons

In the island of Jamaica in the West Indies some runaway slaves, chiefly Asante, formed a state of their own in the mountains in the seventeenth century. They were known as Maroons. They were such good fighters that the Jamaican Government could not bring them back and had to let them stay where they were.

Some of these Maroons began fighting the Jamaican Government again in 1795. Eventually they agreed to make peace, on condition that they might stay in their homes. But the promise was disregarded, and about five hundred of them were deported to Nova Scotia.

There they were as cold and unhappy as the Nova Scotians had been and demanded to go somewhere else. At last the Sierra Leone Company agreed to take them. In return, the British Government promised to give money for a fort to defend Freetown and soldiers to garrison it.

The Nova Scotian Rebellion

The Nova Scotians had many grievances; in particular they resented having to pay rent for their land. Clarkson had promised them that they would receive it free of charge. But the Company insisted that a small annual rent must be paid.

Some of them began to feel that they must get rid of the Company's government and govern themselves. Already they elected their own representatives every year to keep order and suggest new laws. They felt these representatives were capable of governing the country.

Four senior representatives voiced this feeling — Isaac Anderson, James Robertson, Nathaniel Wansey and Ansel Zizer. Anderson was a carpenter, long hostile to the government; unlike most Nova Scotians, he had been born free. Robertson, an elderly man, was a spirit dealer. Wansey and Zizer were farmers (Wansey's farm, Wansey Hill, was on the present Tower Hill). In September 1800 they announced that the Company's laws were no longer in force and issued new laws of their own.

As this was defiance of government, the Governor, Thomas Ludlam, sent some men to arrest them, and there was a struggle. Robertson and Zizer were captured, but Anderson and Wansey got away and gathered their armed followers next day east of the town.

About fifty Nova Scotians joined Anderson; about thirty joined Ludlam. Most remained neutral. They were lawabiding people, but they were not going to fight for a government they mistrusted. So things looked bad for Ludlam, encamped on Thornton Hill.

Suddenly a ship was seen approaching the harbour. It was the ship carrying the Maroons, with a detachment of British soldiers on board. Ludlam was saved. The Maroons gladly agreed to help their new government, and they and the soldiers easily defeated the rebels. Wansey escaped, but Anderson and one of his followers, Francis Patrick, were tried and hanged. The other leaders were banished.

After the rebellion the Nova Scotians were no longer allowed to elect representatives for fear they would again challenge the Company. They and the Maroons were ruled from England without being given any say in the government.

CHAPTER EIGHT
Temne under pressure

The Koya Temne and the Company

Naimbana died in 1793. One of his sons, John Henry, was in England being educated by the Company. He returned after his father's death but fell ill on the voyage and died. His relatives were angry; it took a long time to persuade them that he had not been killed — indeed some of them were never persuaded.

A king of the Koya Temne was elected after Naimbana's death with the title Bai Farama. Naimbana had been the Company's landlord; Bai Farama appointed King Jimmy landlord. When King Jimmy died in 1796, his successor, who took the name King Tom, also became landlord.

The Company's officials did not understand or obey the rules of landlord and stranger (see pages 17–18). If one of the settlers was involved in a dispute outside, they settled it themselves instead of leaving it to the landlord. They did not pay the landlord rent. When the landlord died, they refused to make a new treaty with his successor, saying that he was already bound by the treaty of 1788.

By English law they were right. Naimbana promised in 1788 on behalf of himself and his successors to give up any claim to the land for ever. So by English law the land belonged to the Company. But by Temne law a stranger only had a right to land so long as his agreement with his landlord lasted. Strangers were not given land for ever.

When the Temne chiefs realized what had happened, they accused the Company of taking their land. The Governor could only reply that no one had forced them to make the treaty, and that they had only themselves to blame for making it. But they could not be satisfied with such an answer and came to look on the Company as an enemy rather than (as it was at first) a friend.

King Tom attacks Freetown

When Bai Farama and King Tom saw soldiers in Freetown and watched them preparing to build a stone fort on Thornton Hill they were alarmed. Wansey who had taken refuge with them, warned them that if they let the fort be built they would never be safe from the British. So they decided to attack.

Early on the morning of 18 November 1801, the Koya Temne forces, led by Wansey, crossed over from King Tom's country to surprise Thornton Hill from the west. The defenders were unprepared. But as shots rang out the soldiers woke up, and the Nova Scotians hurried out to defend their homes. There was a hard struggle before they finally charged, headed by the Governor, and drove the invaders back into King Tom's country.

Then a counter-attack was prepared. A British naval officer who was sailing down the coast sent some sailors to help, and Ngombu Smart sent some of his Loko army. They invaded King Tom's country and drove the Temne and Bulom out of every town and village west of Freetown.

King Tom took refuge with Mandinka and Susu chiefs north of the Scarcies. Some of them took his side. They waited until the British sailors had gone and attacked Freetown again, this time from the east. But they were again unsuccessful, and were driven off after only twenty minutes' fighting.

Still unwilling to admit defeat, King Tom found new allies, and encamped on the Bulom Shore waiting for another chance to attack.

The Nova Scotians were afraid to go out to their farms. They gathered in Freetown where they and the Maroons built stone walls round the town and a stone fort, Fort Thornton. The town walls were later pulled down, but the fort is still standing. A stone tower was also built on Wansey Hill, renamed Tower Hill. Part of it is still standing with a water tank inside it.

Just before the Temne war began, a Susu trader, Dala Modu, came to settle in Freetown with about fifty followers. His father was an important man in Susu country and his family had gained great influence. In 1803 he persuaded King Tom's allies to go home. King Tom, left all alone, had to give up the struggle and abandon his country.

The peace treaty

Not until July 1807 did the Koya Temne make a final peace treaty. As they had been defeated they had to accept the British terms — that they give up all the land west of Freetown and the waterfront towns east of it.

These years were desperate years for the coastal Temne. The British had driven them from most of the peninsula. Ngombu Smart encroached on them in the Rokel country. They had lost control of Port Loko where Braima Konkuri, the usurping chief who ruled there, boasted that in ten years there would not be one Temne left in the country.

CHAPTER NINE
The Crown Colony

The Anti-Slave Trade Act

After years of campaigning an act was passed by the British Parliament
in 1807, forbidding British subjects to trade in slaves, or anyone to
trade in slaves in a British colony. But it was only a step towards abolishing the slave trade. It affected only the British, not other Europeans,
so the trade went on.

The British Crown takes over

The Sierra Leone Company had lost so much money that it could no
longer afford to support the settlement, so the British Government
agreed to take it over. On 1 January 1808, the Company's flag was pulled
down in Freetown and the British flag, the Union Jack, put up. This
showed that the settlement was now a British Crown Colony, under
the King of Great Britain.

A Governor was sent to rule as the King's representative. He took
orders from the Secretary of State in London, and sent him regular
accounts of everything he did. If the Secretary of State disapproved of
something he had done, he had to change it. He had a small Council to
advise him, consisting chiefly of senior officials. Laws were made in
the name of the Governor and Council. But if the members disagreed
with him, the Governor could ignore them and make his own laws in
their name.

So in those days the Governor could do very much as he liked. The
Secretary of State was far off in London. There were only slow sailing
ships to carry their correspondence. Each new Governor did what he
thought best — which was often quite different from what the last
governor had done. In Freetown they used to say, 'New Governor,
new law.'

The Colony in 1808

In 1808 the whole population was under two thousand. Most were 'Settlers' — that is, Nova Scotians and Maroons. Each lived in their own part of Freetown, the Nova Scotians from Little East Street to Charlotte Street, the Maroons west of Charlotte Street. They disliked one another. The Nova Scotians could not forget how the Maroons had put down their rebellion. But they lived peaceably side by side without fighting.

Few Nova Scotians returned to the farms they had left after the Temne war, and the land reverted to bush. Nor did the Maroons farm. Most Settlers became traders; some became government clerks. The Government Printer was James Wise, a young Nova Scotian who had learnt printing in England. Those who were masons and carpenters built houses to live in or let to European officials. As house rents brought in a good income, it became usual for any Settler who had made a bit of money by trading to build a house to let.

Their houses were mostly wooden frames, raised off the ground on a stone cellar to keep out insects and the damp, with a stone staircase. Visitors from up-country were amazed to see houses up in the air.

Several of the best houses were owned by women. Some of the Nova Scotian women were enterprising traders who opened shops in Freetown or went to trade in the rivers. Mrs Sophia Small, one of the first to open a shop, made enough to build a house valued at £900; she owned other houses too. They were inherited by her daughter Jane, who married a European carpenter, George Nicol, who then became a prosperous trader.

There were only about twenty or thirty European residents. Most were officials, the rest traders. There was only one big trading firm, Macaulay and Babington, started by Zachary Macaulay after he ceased to be employed by the Sierra Leone Company. The Freetown manager was his relative, Kenneth Macaulay.

There was also a small group of men from the Kru Coast, about five hundred kilometres to the south. Kru men were noted for being good sailors. They would leave home as boys, work perhaps twenty or thirty years on the coast as sailors or harbour labourers, then return home. In 1793 they started coming to Freetown, where they lived together in their own Kru Town.

After the Temne war, Temne chiefs stopped sending their children to school. But many Temne and Bulom came regularly to trade or to work as labourers and servants. Some sent children to work in a Settler's family where they could learn new ways.

Europeans ruled, but it was not a European colony. The Settlers, the largest group, were not of European descent. They spoke their own style of English, different from that spoken in England. Some Europeans thought them more like Africans. But though their dances and some of their customs were African in origin, they had been changed by their residence in America. They were Christians and attended their own churches regularly. To the Temne and Bulom they were more like Europeans. Thus they formed a separate, distinctive group, neither wholly African nor wholly European.

CHAPTER TEN
The coastal region in the early nineteenth century

The Gallinas country

The Gallinas country, round the Moa and Mano estuaries, was an important slave-trading centre. The coastal chiefs, particularly the Massaquoi and Rogers families, controlled the slave trade and grew rich. King Siaka, the head of the Massaquoi, living at Gendama, sometimes employed European clerks to do his business for him.

Traders who came from inland to the Gallinas country were not allowed to deal directly with Europeans (see pages 17–18). They had to trade through the coastal chiefs who took a large commission. The inland peoples resented this system, and for many years there were constant wars between them and the people on the coast.

A Coup at Port Loko

In 1815 a secret society was started in Port Loko to drive out Braima Konkuri and the usurping Susu chiefs (see pages 16, 33). It was organized by Moriba Bangura, who was himself of Susu origin, and was a Muslim. Once when he was trading in the north, he had taken the title Ailkali (a form of the Arabic word for a judge).

When the signal was given they rose. Braima was defeated, and his head cut off. Moriba became ruler of Port Loko, with the title Alikali, under the overlordship of Bai Foki, the Temne King.

The timber trade

Round Freetown most of the big trees were cut down to build houses. But trees of up to thirty metres high grew all over the surrounding country. A young Irish trader, John McCormack, realized that they could be turned into money. Ships were still built of wood then. He saw that these tall, strong trees would make excellent ship's timber and

37

decided to cut them down for export to England.

He and other traders settled on the islands in the Port Loko Creek. They employed Kru labourers to cut down the trees on the banks and float them over to be prepared for sale. Eventually the logs were taken to England to be used for ship-building.

The neighbouring chiefs were delighted. Since the Anti-Slave Trade Act no slaves had been exported from the Port Loko Creek or Rokel, for the Colony Government prevented it. The slave-traders had moved away, and the chiefs lost their rents and their supply of goods. The timber traders brought business back, built timber depots, and paid the chiefs rent for them in the old way. Goods were available for timber now instead of slaves.

Temne labourers also began working in the timber trade. They received regular wages (which they did not get from their chiefs), paid in goods. So the timber trade spread prosperity through the country. But the prosperity was not permanent. The timber traders cut down the trees but planted no new ones. In any case it takes centuries for a really big tree to grow. Once all the big trees in an area were felled, they moved to another, until the whole country was gradually deforested.

Dala Modu

Dala Modu, who had helped the Company against King Tom, lived with his people in Freetown until 1806. Then the Governor accused him of slave-trading and ordered him to appear and explain himself. Dala Modu, when in Freetown, usually dressed like a European. But he appeared before the Governor defiantly in a Muslim gown, as if to show he cared nothing for him. The Governor ordered him out.

He crossed with his people to the Bulom Shore. The Bulom chiefs let him settle at Lungi, where he built a town with stone houses like those in Freetown. He went on trading successfully. When the timber trade started he made his people cut down trees, which he sold at a good profit in Freetown. Soon he was more powerful than the Bulom chiefs, who did little trading. When he died in 1841 he had made himself the most important chief in the country.

CHAPTER ELEVEN
The era of Governor MacCarthy

The recaptives

The Anti-Slave Trade Act empowered British naval ships to capture slave ships and bring them before a British court for trial.—

The freed slaves were called 'recaptives', because they had first been captured and made slaves, then captured again and made free. The Government had to consider what to do with them. One ship might be filled with people from the Congo (today, Zaire) over three thousand kilometres to the south; the next might be from Senegal, about eight hundred kilometres to the north. Recaptives could not be sent back to such distant homes where in any case they would probably be sold again. So they were kept in the Colony. As there were too many to stay in Freetown, they were sent to found villages nearby.

Fig 6 Freetown Prison (built 1815) and the gate into the Liberated African Yard where recaptives were taken on arrival (photograph taken in 1870)

39

Leicester village, in the mountains behind Freetown, was the first, started by recaptives from the Wolof and Bambara countries. A group of Congo recaptives was sent to a deserted Temne village in the hills west of Freetown, but they preferred the waterside and moved down and built their own Congo Town by the shore. Another group settled east of Freetown at Kissy; they are supposed to have come from the Kise-Kise River north of Sierra Leone. Another group, who spoke Portuguese, founded Portuguese Town on the outskirts of Freetown on a site where there had been a Temne village under a headman called Pa Demba (Pademba Road is named after him). Others settled in the mountains.

Every year hundreds of recaptives were brought in. By 1815 over six thousand had been landed. Some, instead of being sent to found villages, were enlisted as soldiers in the British army. Others, particularly the children, became servants or apprentices to Settlers and Europeans.

Christian missionaries

Towards the end of the eighteenth century Christian missions revived (see page 12). Christians in Europe began to feel that it was their duty to spread their religion over the whole world. Societies were founded, supported by voluntary contributions, to sponsor missionary work.

During the 1790s a few Protestant missionaries came to preach in Sierra Leone. But they had no proper training or previous experience. They all fell ill and died, or went away discouraged.

In 1799 the Church Missionary Society (CMS), a Church of England institution, was founded in London, to train missionaries properly. Missions were still regarded as something strange, and no Englishman wanted to train. The CMS found Germans instead. Melchior Renner, Leopold Butscher and Gustavus Nyländer were among the first. They went to the Rio Pongas, to try and convert the Susu to Christianity.

Some of the Nova Scotian Methodists decided they would like a European to help them. They wrote to England, and the Wesleyan Missionary Society (later renamed Methodist Missionary Society) sent them a missionary, the Rev George Warren.

Governor MacCarthy and the recaptives

Charles MacCarthy, a British army officer of part-French, part-Irish descent, took charge of the Colony in 1814, and in 1816 was formally appointed Governor. He dreamed of transforming it into a centre from which Christianity and European ways would flow out all over West Africa.

He was shocked to find that the recaptives were just being dumped down in villages with no one to teach them or look after them. He persuaded the CMS to leave the Rio Pongas and concentrate on turning the recaptives into Christians. He wanted a missionary in charge of every village, not just preaching to the people but keeping them in order as a government superintendent.

The most famous missionary superintendent was the Rev William Johnson of the CMS, who looked after Regent village. He found the people divided and disorganized. They came from many different places — some were Ibo (from what is today Nigeria), some Bulom, some Susu, and there were many others from other parts of the coast. How was he to unite these people into one community?

Johnson found that the recaptives were responsive to Christianity. They felt cut off from the religions they had known in their distant homelands. As they came from many different countries, they had to learn English to speak to one another — and English was the language Christians spoke. In Freetown they saw Settlers — prosperous, well-dressed Christians, an example to imitate. So they were ready to listen to Christian preaching and adopt the ways associated with it, such as European-style clothes and European names.

A church was built at Regent — the first stone church in the Colony. As superintendent, Johnson could make the people go to church, but

Fig 7 Regent village at the time of the Reverend W. A. B. Johnson

most were glad to go without being forced. Soon Regent was full of Christians.

Some missionaries gave the recaptives new names, but most preferred to choose names for themselves. So, though many had missionary names (like Renner or Metzger), far more had names of officials (like MacCarthy, Reffell, Nicol, Coker or Macfoy). Some took Settler names (like Williams, Jarrett or Davis). Many took the name Macaulay, from Kenneth Macaulay, the leading European trader.

The Government built schools in the villages. The CMS also had a Christian Institution on Leicester Mount, founded in 1814, to train recaptive teachers and missionaries. It was moved to Regent and the Leicester building became a recaptive hospital. So many diseases broke out on the crowded slave-ships that the recaptives were often landed sick and had to be sent straight to hospital.

John Macaulay Wilson, a Bulom whose father was king of the Bulom Shore, was in charge of the hospital. As a boy he had been sent to England by the Sierra Leone Company and trained as a druggist. On his return he settled in Freetown, married a Maroon, and practised medicine. He was elected king to succeed his father, but died two weeks after his election.

The British Government persuaded some other European governments to combine to put down the slave trade. An international court with judges from different European nations, was opened in Freetown where slave-ships belonging to those nations could be brought.

But still the slave trade went on. Brazil and Cuba were being developed for sugar-growing. Thousands of slaves were needed for the sugar plantations. So the illegal slave trade continued, and every year thousands of new recaptives were settled in MacCarthy's villages.

MacCarthy in Freetown

MacCarthy loved building. He got the superintendents to build churches and government buildings in the villages (the ruins of the government buildings can still be seen at York and Kent). In Freetown he enlarged the wharf and built stone steps down to it (they are sometimes called the 'Portuguese Steps', but they have nothing to do with the Portuguese). Many of the buildings he put up lasted until the twentieth century.

They had to be paid for by the British Government, for the revenue of the Colony, chiefly from customs duties, was only a few thousand pounds a year. The British Government usually grudged spending money on distant colonies, but MacCarthy was a persuasive man and induced it to pour out hundreds of thousands of pounds for his schemes.

As Freetown grew European traders were attracted there. The timber trade, too, was an attraction, so the population increased. The Settlers built houses for these new European immigrants. It was estimated that a Settler who spent £600 building a house could let it for £120 a year — a good investment for his money. New stone houses went up in every street. There were eighty in 1818, one hundred and seventeen in 1823. New streets were laid out east and west.

MacCarthy liked people to enjoy themselves. He gave dinners and dances and encouraged others to do the same. In Christmas Week there was a fair with entertainments and horse-racing. A racecourse was laid out at Fourah Bay (where Race Course Road still commemorates it).

The expanding Colony

After Britain and France made peace in 1815 the British army was reduced, and African soldiers who had served in British regiments were pensioned and sent to the Colony. MacCarthy put some (who had served at Gibraltar) just east of Freetown, where they founded Gibraltar Town.

Some Temne were still living in the eastern part of the peninsula. MacCarthy made a treaty with their chiefs, who gave up their right to the peninsula in return for an annual payment. Pensioned soldiers were sent to start villages there — Wellington, Hastings and Waterloo. Others went to York and Kent on the Atlantic shore. Once they were settled in, recaptives were sent to join them.

MacCarthy also persuaded the Caulkers to lease the Banana Islands for an annual rent. Recaptives were settled there. Thomas Caulker moved to Bumpe on the mainland.

MacCarthy wanted to stimulate trade with the countries inland and sent a European officer with a friendly message to the ruler of Futa Jalon. Another officer, Captain Gordon Laing, travelled up the Rokel and beyond it to Falaba. The people in these countries had never had a European visitor before. One chief wanted to know whether he had bones in his body. At Falaba the king was delighted to meet him, but refused to let him go further inland.

These visits encouraged traders to visit Freetown. Fula and Mandinka traders often travelled in large groups, called 'caravans', coming overland to Port Loko or to Magbele, a trading centre on the Rokel belonging to a Temne king, Bai Koblo, where they would get into canoes for Freetown.

A few Fula and Mandinka settled in Freetown. They acted as land-lords for their countrymen when they came to trade, explaining unfamiliar ways for them and selling their goods on commission. They settled east of the town at Foulah Town, where they built a mosque.

In 1821 all the British West African colonies were united. MacCarthy was put in charge of them, with Freetown as the capital, but he could not control such a wide area, which stretched from the Gambia to Accra, so the officials in the other colonies did what they liked. He went to Cape Coast and found them preparing to fight the Asante. He knew nothing of the circumstances but agreed in his cheerful way to lead the army. In January 1824 they met the Asante army at Nsamanko; MacCarthy was killed and his army annihilated.

After this the British Government realized it was impossible for one governor to rule such a wide area properly. So in 1827 the colonies were divided again.

CHAPTER TWELVE
Bulom and Temne country in the 1820s

The Sherbro Treaty

As the slave trade still continued across the Atlantic, the kings and chiefs in the Sherbro and Gallinas countries went on supplying slaves to European traders. A British naval squadron sailed up and down the coast to capture slave ships, but it could not hope to capture them all. Slave ships would hide up a river till the naval ship had gone past, then hurry out and sail across the Atlantic.

The Caulker and Cleveland families were still at war. In 1825 Chief George Caulker asked Governor Turner, MacCarthy's successor, to come and make peace. Turner sailed to the Plantain Islands, where all the Sherbro rulers were gathered. He told them that before he made peace they must first give up their countries to the British. They agreed, and a treaty was made.

The Government in London was alarmed by what Turner had done. They remembered MacCarthy, who had dreamed of great empires and had got himself killed and his army destroyed. They wanted no more West African adventures. Turner was told to give the rulers back their country, and was warned not to annex any more of West Africa.

It made no difference to the Sherbro rulers. They had only agreed with Turner out of politeness, and had never had any intention of giving up their independence.

The Port Loko election of 1825

Alikali Moriba Bangura of Port Loko died in 1825, having nominated his friend Fatima Brima Kamara to succeed him as Alikali. This was an unpopular choice; many Port Loko people supported another candidate, Pa Runia. Fatima Brima had connections with the British, as his brother was agent for Kenneth Macaulay. Macaulay was the richest businessman in Freetown and a member of the Governor's Council. Fatima Brima asked for his support.

Macaulay agreed to help him, and told Governor Turner that there was going to be a war over the succession, and that they must intervene to keep the peace. So Turner was persuaded to go with Macaulay and a party of soldiers to Port Loko where they had Fatima Brima crowned. From now on it was accepted that the Governor of Sierra Leone or his representative should crown a new Alikali.

The Temne-Loko War

When the slave trade from the Rokel ceased, Ngombu Smart, who had grown rich through it, lost much of his power. His successor, also Ngombu Smart, could not afford to make large payments to Bai Simera, in whose country he lived, so Bai Simera wanted to get rid of him. They quarrelled and submitted their dispute to Alikali Fatima Braima, who decided against Smart.

Smart and his Loko followers rejected this decision. All the neighbouring Temne then joined to drive them out. He was killed but his family went on fighting, helped by Mende chiefs to the south. The Temne overran the Loko towns; many Loko took refuge in the Colony.

A party of British officials went to Port Loko in 1831 to mediate. The Loko submitted and were allowed back to some of their towns. The Temne chiefs made a treaty promising not to make war in the future without consulting the Governor, and in return the British Government paid them an annual sum of money or 'stipend'. If they made war without permission they would not be paid.

In succeeding years many similar treaties were made with neighbouring chiefs, promising stipends in return for peace. Sometimes the stipendiary chief was given a medal. But the system never worked very well. Most chiefs who wanted to make war did so without consulting the Governor, while the stipends, which were supposed to be paid yearly, were often neglected for years on end.

The Temne victory

Despite the treaty, Temne and Loko went on fighting. Gradually the Loko were driven north and finally entrenched themselves at Kasona, a stronghold on the Mabole River.

Recaptive farmers often moved across the frontier into Koya, where they were beyond the control of the Government. They were also beyond its protection, for the Government refused to protect those who left the Colony. Many of them were Mende recaptives who made contact with their Mende countrymen inland. The Koya Temne were alarmed, fearing they would be encircled — Mende on one side, Mende recaptives on the other.

Temne country was full of small armies who were helping to fight the Loko. Suddenly they started attacking the immigrants in Koya, plundering their farms, seizing them and selling them. About fifteen hundred were killed or sold. They begged the Government to help them, but were told they had only themselves to blame if they strayed across the frontier. Eventually John McCormack, who had started the timber trade, went to mediate. He had lived many years among the Temne; they liked and respected him, and promised not to molest the farmers again.

Alikali Fatima Braima died in 1841. The governor went to crown his successor Namina Modu, a son of the first Alikali, from the Bangura family. It now became the custom to choose alternately a Bangura or a Kamara (Fatima Braima's family). But they were still under the overlordship of Bai Foki (see page 37).

Then began the final Temne onslaught on the Loko. At last Kasona was taken and Loko power broken. The Loko were driven into a few chiefdoms beyond the Mabole. Many took refuge in the Colony. The Smart family, however, were allowed to stay in Temne country at Mahera.

So the Temne, who a few years earlier had been threatened with extinction, were now the predominant people in the Rokel country and north of it.

CHAPTER THIRTEEN
The rise of the recaptives

The recaptive villages

During the 1820s and 1830s thousands of recaptives were landed every year. New villages were started for them. Leicester Hospital was closed and a new hospital built at Kissy, with an isolation ward at the waterfront where recaptives with smallpox and other infectious diseases could be landed.

The CMS could not supply enough superintendents so the government put in officials called 'Managers' instead. When new recaptives arrived the Manager gave them clothes and rations for six months. They then had to look after themselves. Most found someone from their own homeland to help them.

During the 1820s there was constant warfare in the Yoruba country of what is now Nigeria. Thousands of Yoruba, enslaved during these wars, were shipped for sale across the Atlantic. Many were rescued by British naval ships and brought to Sierra Leone. They formed the largest group of recaptives. They were known as 'Aku'[1].

In most villages there were groups from each recaptive nation. Each national group tended to stick together, recognizing one of its members as headman, and obeying his orders. The Aku, the largest group, as well as village headmen, had their own 'king' whom all Aku were supposed to obey. Thomas Will was king in the 1830s.

The recaptives also started 'Companies', benevolent societies whose members looked after one another in sickness, and buried those who died. They also helped one another build houses and make farms. The Companies made rules and the members had to obey them.

The villages were usually peaceful. The Government imagined the Managers kept them quiet, but in fact the people were really ruled by their own government of headmen and Companies.

---

[1] Today the word 'Aku' is only used for Muslims of Yoruba descent. Originally it was used for all Yoruba recaptives.

A village Manager flogged John Langley, an Ibo receptive teacher, and Langley brought an action for assault. The Manager said receptives had no right to bring actions against him. The Chief Justice decided for Langley, and the Manager had to pay damages. This case showed receptives that the law was their friend, and that in the law-courts they had equal rights with Europeans.

The recaptives become Christians

European missionaries of the CMS and the Methodist Mission made many converts among the recaptives. So did Settler preachers. Soon there was scarcely a village in the Colony that did not have at least one church. Some villages had several.

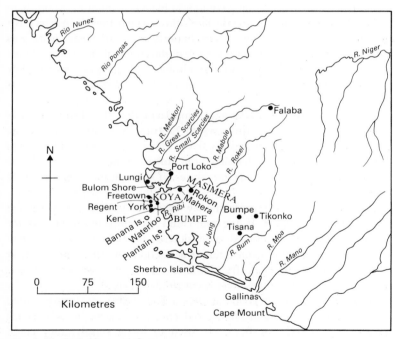

Map 2 The Early Nineteenth Century

European missionaries and Settler pastors often found it difficult to make recaptives understand their message. So they divided their congregations into 'classes'. Each class had a class-leader, a converted recaptive, in charge. These class-leaders could speak to their own people in a way the missionaries could not. So in villages where there was no missionary or pastor the Christian gospel was preached by recaptive class-leaders.

Just as the Managers relied on recaptive headmen and Companies to govern the villages, so the missionaries relied on recaptive class-leaders to make them Christian.

The recaptives grow rich

The recaptives wanted to make money like the Europeans and Settlers. They farmed in their villages, but there was little demand for produce. What they sold only provided enough to live on without enabling them to live better, so the more ambitious among them moved to Freetown seeking work. But there were few opportunities: domestic work was done by recaptive apprentices; Kru men did much of the heavy labour. So they cut firewood to sell and did odd jobs, and with the pennies they earned bought goods from the shops and hawked them in the streets as petty traders.

In 1835 the British Parliament, impatient that the slave trade was still continuing, allowed the navy to capture ships fitted out for the slave trade, even if they had no slaves on board. Ships were brought into Freetown full of bales of cotton, tobacco and spirits which the owners had meant to trade for slaves. These cargoes were publicly auctioned.

Recaptives who had made money by street trading began buying up these bargain goods. If one man could not afford to bid enough for them himself, he combined with others. Several recaptives would pool their savings, buy a consignment at auction, and share it out among themselves. Thomas Will, the Aku king, spent £50 at an auction; next year he spent over £100. Others spent similar sums.

With large stocks of goods at their disposal they no longer traded in the streets. They built shops and employed agents to take goods up-country to sell. As they were used to living simply, they could afford to charge low prices and undersell European and Settler shopkeepers. Within a few years many, who perhaps only a decade before had been penniless slaves, were buying and selling hundred of pounds' worth of goods every year.

50

The Seventeen Nations

The recaptives had come from many nations. Even after ten or twenty years some still felt national differences strongly. In Christmas Week 1843 a riot broke out at Waterloo between the Aku and Ibo. After it was put down, John Macaulay went to make peace. He was a trader of forceful character and independent views who had succeeded Thomas Will as Aku king.

Macaulay persuaded the seventeen largest national groups in Waterloo to combine to settle disputes between peoples of different nations. Each group appointed representatives who met together under the name of the 'Seventeen Nations'. Similar committees were started in other villages. This united the recaptives and their children more closely.

Rich recaptives

Emmanuel Cline was a Hausa recaptive who started trading in a small way in Freetown, first in the streets, then, after buying goods at auction, in a shop. With his savings he bought an estate at Fourah Bay, divided it into small lots and sold them at a profit for people to build on. It is still called Cline Town. When he died, he left money to build a church there.

A Nupe boy was landed in Freetown in 1827. He was apprenticed to a Frenchman who called him Isadore, but he came to be known as John Ezzidio. He was honest and intelligent, worked as a shop assistant for several Europeans, then, with his savings, started on his own. By 1841 he had made enough to buy a house in George Street for £100. As he was a devout Methodist and preached regularly, a Methodist missionary took him to England and introduced him to business people there. From them he was able to order goods to sell in Freetown. By 1850 he was importing over £3000 worth of goods every year.

William Henry Pratt, an Ibo, also started as a shop assistant and then branched out on his own. He too made contacts with firms in England and imported goods regularly. He took his children to England and left them at school to give them the education he had never had.

Cline, Ezzidio and Pratt are only three examples of many who within a few years raised themselves by their own hard work from poverty to wealth. They filled their houses with expensive imported furniture, ate rich imported food, drank imported wine, and wore fashionable imported clothes — top hats and long coats — to advertise their new grandeur.

Some recaptives return home

Two Hausa men arrived in Freetown from Brazil. They had been slaves, were now free, and were on their way back to the Hausa country. Recaptives began wondering why they too did not return home, now they were rich enough not to fear being enslaved again. Three Aku combined to buy a ship in 1839 and sailed with passengers to the coast of what is now Nigeria. From there they went inland to their old homes.

The Yoruba country, rich and well populated, offered many opportunities for trade. Soon many were leaving Freetown to trade there. Some stayed; others returned when they had made enough money.

This movement of recaptives down the coast had a great effect on Sierra Leone. From now on, when an enterprising man wanted to make money, he was as likely to go overseas as to go inland. Those who were missionaries dreamed of converting their own people, hundreds of miles away, rather than the nearby Bulom and Temne. From the 1840s the Colony began to look outwards along the coast, rather than inwards towards its own hinterland.

Education

In 1827 the CMS institution for training teachers (see page 42), was refounded in premises at Fourah Bay. It was called the Christian Institution. The first pupil was an Aku, Samuel Ajayi Crowther. When he left the Institution he became a mission teacher.

The CMS realized how much the recaptives could do to make West Africa Christian. Crowther was brought to England, and ordained as a clergyman. He then returned to the Yoruba country, his old home, as a missionary. There he met his mother and relatives, who were amazed to find the boy they had long ago supposed vanished for ever into slavery, returning with all the dignity and attainments of a European gentleman. Eventually he was made a bishop.

Encouraged by his success, the CMS enlarged the Christian Institution, and put up a new four-storey building at Fourah Bay, where not only teachers but missionaries could be trained.

In 1845 the CMS opened a grammar school in Freetown. This was not a missionary institution but a school providing secondary education. It was not meant only for the Colony: the first names on the school register included two boys from the Gallinas country and one Temne. Boys were also sent there from other parts of West Africa.

The CMS opened a girls' secondary school in 1849. It was known as

Fig 8 The original building of the Christian Institution at Fourah Bay

Fig 9 The new building of the Christian Institution, later known as Fourah Bay College

53

the Female Institution until 1877 when it was renamed the Annie Walsh Memorial School.

Fig 10 The Annie Walsh Memorial School

The Methodist missionaries opened an institution on King Tom peninsula to train ministers and missionaries. The Rev Charles Knight, an Ibo, and the Rev Joseph Wright, an Aku, were the first recaptives they ordained.

Muslim recaptives

Some recaptives, particularly the Aku, were Muslims and retained their own religion. The Government was suspicious of them, but they were protected by a lawyer, W. H. Savage, who let them settle on his land at Fourah Bay (still known as 'Savage Square'). Others joined the Fula and Mandinka at Fula Town, soon outnumbering them. There were also Muslims at Murray Town, Aberdeen, Hastings and other villages.

Many Christians disliked them and accused them of kidnapping and other crimes. In 1839 there was a riot against them, and the Fourah Bay mosque was pulled down. There was talk of turning them out of the country, but the Government decided against it, and the mosque was rebuilt.

Some went back to Yoruba country, but most stayed where they were, in East Freetown or the villages. Though they were divided from the rest of the Aku community by their religion they still retained close ties of friendship and marriage with them. But they tended to live apart in their own communities, with their own interests and local politics, educating their children in Koranic schools, and sometimes sending them to Futa Jalon for higher education.

CHAPTER FOURTEEN
Trading in vegetable produce

The groundnut trade

When the trees were cut down round the Rokel and Port Loko Creek, and only bush remained, unsuited for shipbuilding, the timber traders moved (see pages 37–8). Some went to the Melakori River, north of the Scarcies; others began cutting to the south.

By far the richest trader in Freetown was Charles Heddle. His father was a European doctor, his mother an African from Senegal. He imported goods and exported produce on a large scale, with big premises in Water Street.

If groundnuts are pressed tightly together, a fine oil comes out of them. At this time many new kinds of machines were being invented in Europe; they needed oil to make them run smoothly. Heddle thought of using groundnut oil and began exporting groundnuts to Europe. Groundnut oil was soon in great demand. By 1847, ten years after the first groundnuts were exported from Sierra Leone, over £20 000 worth were being exported annually.

Groundnuts grow plentifully along the rivers north of Sierra Leone. Heddle had a depot at the mouth of the Melakori, where they were collected and shipped to Freetown to be exported Europe. After hearing that a French naval ship was in the area he feared that the French might take the country and spoil his trade.

The Governor at that time was William Fergusson, a West Indian of part-African descent who had served many years in Freetown as an army doctor. He was a wise, capable man, who was loved and trusted. In 1845 he was made Governor — the only time the British Government ever appointed a Governor of African descent.

He agreed with Heddle that British influence ought to extend over the groundnut-producing area, to keep out the French. But the British Government, ever since Turner's time, had refused to let the Colony be enlarged, or take any new territories (see page 45). All he could do was to make treaties of friendship. So the rulers as far north as the Rio Nunez made treaties, promising friendship, and receiving annual stipends.

56

Palm produce

Palm oil was used in Europe to make soap and candles. (Electric light had not yet been invented, so many people still relied on candles for light.) Traders in the Sherbro country, rich in oil palms, exported it. By the 1840s exports of palm oil were beginning to rival timber.

Heddle, with his usual foresight, noticed that the palm kernels, which were thrown away when the oil was boiled out, contained a fine oil. Instead of throwing them away he began exporting palm kernels to Europe. They too brought him large profits. Others soon followed his example.

Trade expands

Trade was still conducted by exchange of goods, as it had always been (see pages 6–9). The trader gave goods, not cash, for produce, as formerly for slaves. The goods supplied were those in demand in West Africa for centuries — cottons, tobacco, spirits, guns and gunpowder.

Recaptive traders moved into the produce-growing areas. Some were petty traders who had bought a small stock of goods with their savings. Some were agents for the newly-rich recaptive shopkeepers. Chiefs were inclined to welcome them (as they had once welcomed the slave-traders) because they brought trade. They settled down in the usual way as strangers, paying the landlord his customary rent. But they were far more numerous than the slave-traders had ever been, and their landlords found it difficult to stop them interfering in political matters.

Dressing and behaving like European traders, they were known as 'white men.' If they quarrelled with a chief, they made a complaint to the Governor in Freetown. Some Governors listened and took the traders' side. But most Governors took little notice, knowing how often these quarrels were provoked by the traders themselves.

The CMS mission to the Temne

By 1840 most of the recaptives had become Christians. The CMS decided to try to convert some of the neighbouring peoples. A mission was opened at Port Loko by the Rev Christian Schlenker.

Schlenker studied the Temne language and published books on it. He also published a book of Temne traditions and stories. But the Port

Loko people were not interested in the religion he preached. Muslims had long been settled there, and those who gave up their own religion usually preferred Islam to Christianity. So the CMS moved from Port Loko to Magbele on the Rokel.

CHAPTER FIFTEEN
Caulker country and southward

The Caulkers at war

George Stephen Caulker of the Plantain Islands died in 1831, and
his brother Thomas Stephen succeeded. Thomas Caulker of Bumpe
died in 1832 and his brother and successor, Charles, began opening
his country to the timber trade. By the time of his death, ten years later,
timber was being exported on a large scale from the rivers flowing into
Yawry Bay.

Now that the timber trade was replacing the slave trade, Thomas
Stephen found the Plantain Islands of little value. He wanted to get
a foothold on the mainland where the timber was, and fought a long
war against Canre Ba Caulker, Charles's successor, saying he had no
right to be chief. But Canre defeated him and drove him off the Plantains
so he settled at Bendu opposite Sherbro Island.

Traders from Freetown took sides, providing arms; some were
plundered and killed. Thomas Stephen went to Freetown to apologize,
and asked the government to mediate between him and Canre. The
Acting Governor went to the Sherbro in a naval ship and made the two
chiefs agree to divide the country. Canre took what lay north, Thomas
Stephen what lay south, of the Cockboro Creek. Thus Thomas Stephen
secured part of the mainland.

Mende involvement

The Mende people were now spreading over the Sherbro country (see
page 00). In the past they had been peaceable, living in their own states,
farming, hunting and trading, without making large-scale wars. But
as they came more into contact with the coastal peoples, they saw how
the coastal rulers had become rich and powerful through controlling
the import-export trade. Ambitious Mende leaders determined to do
the same. To gain power for themselves, they began organizing their
people for warfare, each leader in rivalry with the other leaders. Soon

59

they gained the reputation of being a military people.

So when the coastal rulers went to war, they called in well-known Mende military leaders and their followers to help them. Both Caulkers enlisted Mende to fight for them. In this way Mende influence spread.

River-heads as trading centres

All the Sierra Leone rivers are blocked by rocks and rapids until between about fifty to sixty kilometres from their mouths. The 'river-heads' where they become navigable were important market centres. Farmers carried in their produce and sold it to traders who shipped it away in canoes or boats. Magbele, for instance, the river-head of the Rokel, was an important town, ruled by Bai Suba, who collected customs duties from the traders on behalf of his overlord Bai Koblo.

The river-heads of the rivers flowing into the Sherbro estuary also became trading centres which grew more important as trade expanded. As well as providing markets for those who bought and sold, they provided wealth and power for the chiefs who ruled them, enabling them to gain revenue by customs duties and taxes. Many disputes arose between rival chiefs trying to get hold of a river-head. They would ask for help from the Mende, usually from one of two inland towns which had a great reputation in war — Bumpe and Tikonko. If Bumpe supported one side, Tikonko would support the other. This was called 'buying war'.

American missionaries

In 1839 a cargo of Mende slaves on board the slave-ship *Amistad* managed to free themselves off the island of Cuba. They killed the captain, and made the crew turn the ship towards Africa again. Eventually, however, they landed up on the coast of the United States. After several law cases it was decided that they were free. In 1841 they returned to their country, accompanied by American missionaries.

The 'Mendi Mission', as it was called, started near the Jong River, on land provided by Chief Harry Tucker. The American missionaries were practical people who were used to working with their hands. They could build a house or a sawmill and were ready to teach their converts to do the same. They refused to have anything to do with spirits or tobacco and would not even use them for trade.

The end of the Sherbro and Gallinas slave trade

The Gallinas country had grown rich on the slave trade. The people would not trouble to grow rice themselves, but bought it from the Sherbro country instead. King Siaka and his son, and successor, Prince Mana, lived in large, well-built houses with expensive furniture imported from Europe. The Rogers family too were rich. James Rogers of Jidaro used to eat off silver plates.

During the 1840s the British naval officers who were trying to suppress the slave trade used a new method. They would land, destroy the slave-trader's premises, and force the chiefs to make treaties giving up the slave trade. The Caulkers and other chiefs in the Sherbro made such treaties. The navy then blockaded the Gallinas estuary, preventing any boat from going in or out.

Fig 11 British naval boats attack the Gallinas slave traders

This cut the Gallinas off from the Sherbro, their food supply. Prince Mana and the Rogers family realized that they would have to give up what had so long been their livelihood. In 1850 they drove out the European slave-traders and made a treaty giving up the slave trade.

The inland people were enraged when they heard they had given up the slave trade, and invaded the coastal area. Without slave-traders to buy arms from, the coastal chiefs were at their mercy. The end of the slave trade meant the end of their long-enjoyed supremacy and prosperity.

Liberia

In 1818 some Americans arrived in Sierra Leone, intending to start a settlement for Americans of African descent. They fixed on a site in the Sherbro country. But it proved unhealthy, so they moved away, and in 1821 founded a new settlement further south. They called it Liberia and their chief town Monrovia.

Many Afro-Americans, former slaves who had gained their freedom, came to settle in Liberia. In 1847 it became an independent state with its own President and Legislature.

As former victims of slavery, the Liberians put down the slave trade in their territories. The British Government was pleased and gave them a small armed ship as a navy. President Roberts, the first President, visited London, where sympathisers gave his government money. With it he made treaties in the Gallinas country, to bring this former centre of the slave trade under Liberian rule and make sure it never revived.

CHAPTER SIXTEEN
British encroachment inland

Steamships

A British firm, the African Steamship Company (which later merged with Elder, Dempster Ltd.), started sending steamships regularly to West Africa in 1852. Until then there had only been sailing ships, which travelled slowly and might stop altogether if the wind dropped.

Steamships brought Sierra Leone in much closer contact with Europe and the rest of West Africa. Traders in Freetown could order goods from England and be sure of getting them in a few weeks. Produce could be shipped quickly to Europe. Steamers held far more than sailing ships, so the volume of trade increased.

The steamships, or mailboats as they were called, for they carried the mails, called at many ports along the coast. Passenger fares were low, so people were encouraged to visit England or other parts of West Africa. Those who did business in the Yoruba country could get there easily. The mailboats carried enterprising adventurers from Sierra Leone to the Gambia, Liberia, the Gold Coast, Lagos, the Oil Rivers south of Lagos, or Fernando Po, seeking their fortune as traders, or offering their services as teachers, missionaries or clerks.

Thomas George Lawson

The Government was regularly in touch with the nearby rulers. There were disputes to be settled, friendly messages to be exchanged (as when a new ruler was installed, or a new Governor arrived), and stipends to be paid. In 1852 a Government Interpreter, Thomas George Lawson, was appointed to carry out these duties.

Lawson came from down the coast from what is today the Republic of Togo. His father, an independent chief, had sent him to Freetown when he was a boy to learn European ways. He lived with John Mc-Cormack, the timber trader, who often took him up country. He became friendly with the Temne chiefs, married a Temne wife, and gained

63

great knowledge of political affairs in the adjoining countries.

Though called an 'Interpreter' he was more like a Minister for Foreign Affairs. All negotiations were carried on through him. When kings and chiefs arrived in Freetown, they lodged at his house, and he took them to see the Governor. Governors always asked his advice, for he knew more of the country than anyone. So until his retirement in 1888 this distinguished African official held a key position in the government.

Maligia and Kambia

When a Governor went on leave, an Acting Governor was appointed to govern for him. Some Acting Governors were excited by their new dignity. They knew it would not last long and made the most of it without considering the consequences.

The chiefs in the Melakori River were annoyed with the British in 1855. They wanted to buy slaves from the Sherbro to plant groundnuts to sell to Freetown traders. But this was slave-trading, so their canoes were captured and the slaves on board freed. Bamba Mina Lahai, chief of Maligia, in retaliation, ordered the traders to leave the country.

They complained to the Acting Governor, Robert Dougan, an Afro-West-Indian lawyer who had lived over twenty years in Freetown. Without consulting the Colonial Office in London or even calling his Council, he decided on immediate war, and sent soldiers in a gunboat to Maligia. Lahai apologized and promised to pay compensation to the traders he had threatened. But as he delayed in paying, Dougan sent a gunboat to destroy Maligia.

When European gunboats attacked an African town, they usually anchored safely a little distance away and fired rockets. The rockets would set the thatched roofs on fire and the town would burn down. This time the officer in charge forgot to bring rockets. Instead the soldiers landed and began striking matches, trying to burn the houses. Suddenly Lahai's people, who had retired into the bush, fired at them. They panicked and rushed back to the boat, where many were drowned trying to get away; others were shot. Altogether seventy-seven were lost. This was the worst disaster the British had ever suffered in Sierra Leone.

When the Governor returned, he was horrified. Governor Hill was an old soldier and was determined to fight another war to restore British prestige.

Kambia was the river-head of the Great Scarcies, where traders from the north arrived overland, and then went on by boat to Freetown. Two chiefs disputed over who should rule it, and war broke out.

Hill decided to intervene to show the people in the Northern Rivers how powerful he was. He took several gunboats up the Scarcies to Kambia. The inhabitants withdrew to the bush, and he burnt the town with rockets. After he had left, the war went on. Next year he took a larger expedition and landed troops, and again the people withdrew. There was no one for him to fight. But he felt proud and happy at having displayed the might of British arms which had been humiliated at Maligia.

The Yoni seek trade

The Yoni, the most southerly of the Temne peoples, lived inland, away from the trading centres. If they wanted trade they had to go to the Rokel, controlled by Masimera and Marampa. The Masimera and Marampa kings got rent from traders, sold timber, and could buy arms and goods. They grew rich, while the Yoni remained poor.

So the Yoni tried to secure a foothold on the Rokel themselves, where traders could come and bring them trade. They fought Masimera and Marampa regularly. In 1860 they attacked Magbele and plundered and destroyed the CMS mission.

Some said the Yoni were hostile to the mission. More likely they supposed the large mission house was a store and plundered it with the other traders' stores. But the CMS never returned. Nor did the Yoni hold Magbele. But they still longed for a trading centre and went on fighting in the hope of winning one.

With so much military experience they became noted soldiers, and, like the Mende of Bumpe and Tikonko, were regularly brought in to take part in wars in the neighbouring countries (see pages 59–60).

The British annex part of the Sherbro

After the slave trade from the Sherbro ceased, the British Government sent a consul to prevent it reviving. But the British did not rule; the country remained independent.

Thomas Stephen Caulker, now established on the mainland, founded a town at Shenge opposite the Plantain Islands. In 1855 American missionaries of the United Brethren in Christ arrived in the Sherbro and Caulker, who was still living at Bendu, let them live at Shenge.

With the slave trade at an end, people began to collect palm produce
to sell to traders. Palm oil and kernels were more easily collected than
timber. As iron ships were now being built in Europe instead of wooden
ships, there was less demand for timber. In any case, most of the fine
forest timber in the coastal country had been cut down and exported,
depriving Sierra Leone of a valuable natural resource.

Traders flocked in from Freetown to buy produce; Bonthe, on
Sherbro Island, became an important trading centre. Heddle had
large premises there. The Mendi Mission headquarters was just across
the swamp at Yandehun.

During the 1850s French traders began settling in the Sherbro. A
French gunboat followed and forced Caulker to sign a treaty promising
to protect them. A French trader complained that he was not being
protected, and a French gunboat anchored off Bendu and bombarded it.
The captain then told Caulker he must leave the town altogether.
French traders boasted that the Sherbro would soon be theirs. In 1861
a French trader announced that he was going to settle at Bendu.

Caulker realized that the days of African sovereignty in the Sherbro

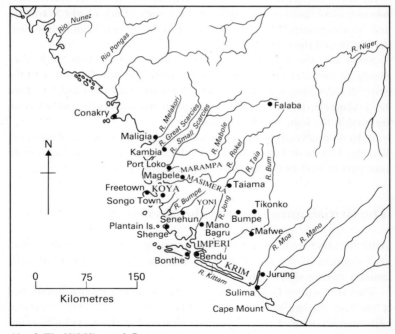

Map 3 The Mid-Nineteenth Century

were coming to an end. He had now to choose which European power should rule there. Rather than surrender to the French he decided to call in the British. He wrote to Governor Hill begging him to annex Bendu as a British territory.

Normally the Government in London refused to annex new territory in West Africa. But for once they let Hill annex Bendu.

Hill was ambitious: one town did not satisfy him. He got Caulker to persuade all the rulers near Bendu, and in the Bagru River, and on Sherbro Island, to offer him their countries. He then went to Bendu, where they all made treaties by which British sovereignty was extended over a large area in the Sherbro.

Most of them imagined they were making treaties of friendship of the usual kind. Not until later did they realize that they had given their countries to the British.

The Koya War

After the loss of the Colony peninsula a curse was put on the Koya kingship so that, when Bai Farama died, no new king was crowned. But John McCormack, always a friend of the Temne, wanted to see Temne rule restored. He got the curse lifted, and in 1859 a son of Bai Farama's was crowned King of Koya under the title Bai Kanta.

Many recaptives lived and traded in western Koya (see pages 46–7). Governor Hill wanted to bring it under British rule. One day in 1861 some Koya people plundered a trader who had taken a Temne man's wife. Hill sent an officer to complain. The officer returned saying he had been insulted, so Hill called out the troops and Bai Kanta hurried to Freetown to apologize. He was told he must pay £300 or else lease part of Koya to the Colony. As he did not have £300 he agreed to lease a strip sixteen kilometres wide for £100 a year.

He believed he was leasing the strip, but the treaty he made (which he could not read) declared it annexed.

In the middle of the leased (or annexed) land lived Songo, a Loko who had been allowed to settle there after the Temne-Loko war. He was often having disputes with his Temne neighbours. Hill sent him a British flag to hoist in his town, told him he was British, and promised him help if any Temne should molest him.

Songo sent a message that he was being attacked, and Hill at once sent troops into Koya. They were joined by Songo with his Loko followers, and a party of Mende under a powerful leader, Gbanya. There was a Temne stockade at Madonkia, which was taken after a short battle; Hill's son, who was leading the attack, was wounded. After that there was little fighting. The troops built a road to Songo Town which became a military headquarters, while their Loko and Mende allies went through Koya burning towns and enslaving the inhabitants.

Early in the following year Bai Kanta made peace — though no one on the British side knew if he had ever made war. He had to give up the strip of land and also his own towns, Robaga and Robana, the sacred towns which had for centuries been the home of the Koya kings.

CHAPTER SEVENTEEN
Political changes

Taxation without representation

Under British colonial rule each colony was supposed to be financially self-supporting. Money to pay for the expenses of government was raised by customs duties and taxation. People in the Sierra Leone Colony had to pay an annual house tax. But they were not allowed to say how the tax money should be spent.

The government was in the hands of the Governor and Council, who sat privately and decided everything themselves. They were responsible to the Colonial Office in London, not to the people. If a law was passed and people disliked it, all they could do was sign a petition of protest which was usually ignored.

Once however a law was made that all street traders should be licensed. There were hundreds of street traders in Freetown, many of them poor people who earned only just enough to live by trading. They said they were too poor to pay for licences, took down their stalls, and announced that if the law was enforced they would leave the Colony. The government was alarmed and said they would not have to pay after all. After this victory the traders in Kissy Street (then called Kissy Road) joined in an association, the Kissy Road Traders' Association, to protect their own interests. It lasted into the twentieth century.

An Afro-West Indian tailor living in Freetown started a newspaper in 1855 called the *New Era*, which voiced the grievances of the unrepresented community. Those who were displeased with the government could write to the *New Era* and complain. Petitions were also sent to London, to the Colonial Office, asking to have a new form of government. But Governor Hill wanted no one to check his powers and advised against making any change.

More and more petitions were sent in, some of them abusive and violent, attacking Hill and other officials. People in the villages were stirred up to demand a new government. Then the rich recaptive shopkeepers were alarmed. The rich are usually afraid of disturbances among the poor, for they fear their own property may be damaged.

They forgot that they wanted a new government and, headed by King Macaulay, sent Hill a petition expressing their deep loyalty to him and the British Government. After this the excitement died down.

A new constitution

In 1863 the Colonial Office decided it was time for a new form of government, or constitution. Hill had been promoted elsewhere, and his successor, Governor Blackall, introduced it.

The Governor's Council was abolished. Instead there was an Executive Council and a Legislative Council. The Executive Council advised the Governor how to rule; all the members were officials. The Legislative Council made the laws; most of the members were officials, but the Governor was told to appoint two non-official members as well, to give the community some share in law-making.

Charles Heddle was one of them. He was so rich (richer than the Governor) that his views could not be ignored. He had for many years sat on the former Governor's Council. Blackall decided to let the leading business men choose the other member, and asked the thirty-nine biggest importers of goods to hold an election. There were two candidates, John Levi, a European, and John Ezzidio (see page 51). The Africans outnumbered the Europeans and their candidate, Ezzidio, was chosen.

So John Ezzidio, who thirty-six years earlier had been a penniless slave, and had raised himself from poverty by hard work and honesty, took his seat on the Legislative Council.

The Colonial Office had not intended that there should be an election. They wanted the Governor to control the Legislative Council and appoint members himself. No more elections were held. In future, when there was a vacancy, the Governor filled it. Nor was the Legislative Council free to make its own laws. Every law had to be sent to London, and if it was not liked it was set aside. Thus the new constitution gave the people little real say in governing their country.

The end of the Atlantic slave trade

All this time the Atlantic slave trade was still going on. The British navy would stop it in one place, but it would spring up in another. One of its last centres was the Rio Pongas, where there are many small rivers connecting with one another. Thick mangrove grows along the banks, so that when a naval ship approached, the slave ships could easily hide till it was gone, or steal out through some unobserved river mouth.

In the early 1860s a final effort was made to stop the slave trade. The United States Government, which had hitherto taken only a small part, began co-operating energetically. In March 1863 a ship with three hundred and sixty-eight slaves on board (one hundred and twenty of them died before they could be freed) was brought into Freetown. Next year two empty slave ships were captured. They were the last. The Atlantic slave trade was at last put down.

The slave trade ceased when it had had outlived its use. Africans could now obtain goods by supplying produce. Europeans were inventing machines which did slaves' work better and more cheaply. So ended the cruel trade which had condemned millions to be brutally transported from their homes, to work like animals for other peoples' profit.

The Parliamentary Committee of 1865

European traders in West Africa did not like being ruled by colonial governments. Though some settled in colonies where they had to obey colonial laws, many preferred living among Africans. From the early days of the slave trade Europeans had lived peaceably under their landlords' protection. They did not want European officials giving them orders. All they wanted was a European governor or naval ship not too far away, for them to call on for help if they had any dispute with their African neighbours.

In England people began wondering if the West African colonies were worth having — the traders did not like them; they were no longer needed to suppress the slave trade; they were unhealthy for Europeans. In 1865 the British Parliament appointed a committee to investigate them. The members recommended against annexing any new territory. They also proposed that the African inhabitants be encouraged to take over the government of the colonies, so that the British could one day withdraw and leave them to rule themselves.

The French in the Northern Rivers

Groundnuts were exported chiefly to France. French people liked to cook with olive oil (English people preferred butter or lard), and groundnut oil was a cheap and palatable substitute. The chiefs in the Melakori River, the centre of the groundnut trade, had made treaties of friendship with the Colony, and many Freetown traders traded there, but the produce went to France.

French officials in Senegal wanted to bring this area of French trade under French control. At first the Government in France was unwilling to interfere in a country so long connected with the British, but after the Parliamentary Committee of 1865 had publicly recommended that there should be no more British annexations in West Africa, the French felt free to act. In 1865 and 1866 they made treaties in the Melakori, Rio Pongas and Roi Nunez, by which the chiefs agreed to put their countries under a French protectorate.

So the policy of 1865 had important consequences for Sierra Leone. Not only were the Northern Rivers lost to the French, but it allowed the people of the Sierra Leone Colony to hope that they would soon achieve self-government.

CHAPTER EIGHTEEN
Freetown at mid-century

Churches and schools

By the middle of the nineteenth century most of the inhabitants of the Sierra Leone Colony were Christians. The CMS realized that such people no longer needed missionaries — indeed some were already missionaries themselves (see page 52), and the CMS felt that they could form their own church. A bishop was appointed, and in 1861 the Native Pastorate Church (later Sierra Leone Church) was founded. The bishop was a European, but the pastors were African. It was governed by committees of clergymen and laymen, part European, part African. Church people were given far more share in running their Church than the government allowed them in running the state.

An African, the Rev James Quaker, was appointed principal of the Grammar School. He was born at Kent village, the son of a disbanded soldier, and educated at the Grammar School and in London. He ran the school efficiently, and the boys did well under him. When he died, the Rev Obadiah Moore, of Mende descent, succeeded him.

The most famous churchman of this time was James Johnson. Born at Benguema of Aku parents, he was educated at the Grammar School and the Fourah Bay Institution, then worked in a Freetown parish. Fearless and outspoken, he never hesitated to say what he believed. He longed for the day when his Church would be completely independent, a true West African Church. From Freetown he was transferred to the Yoruba Mission. Like so many of his countrymen he was lost to Sierra Leone, and his achievements belong to the history of Nigeria.

The Methodist Mission opened a secondary school in 1874, the Methodist Boys' High School. The first principal was the Rev Claudius May, the son of an Aku recaptive, the Rev Joseph May. He was a fine teacher, kind and patient, who won the affection of his staff and pupils, and made his school as good as, if not better than, the Grammar School.

Another girls' secondary school — later called the Methodist Girls' High School — was opened in 1880. James Taylor, a Methodist contractor and shopkeeper, managed it and supported it financially. After his death the Methodist Mission took it on.

Fig 12 Four drawings of Freetown made in about 1840 by Mrs Laetitia Terry. They show the views from the four upstairs windows, one in each direction, of the Liberated African Department premises (later the CMS Grammar School) on the corner of Oxford Street and Wellington Street

Roman Catholic mission

A Roman Catholic Bishop and several priests arrived in Freetown in 1859 to found a mission. Yellow fever broke out; they all caught it and died. In 1864 Father Blanchet, of the Congregation of the Holy Ghost, refounded it more successfully. He was joined by nuns of the Order of St Joseph of Cluny (whose foundress, the Blessed Anne-Marie Javouhey, had visited Freetown in Governor MacCarthy's time). They opened schools, and did much good work among the poor. But unlike the Protestant Churches they did not train up an African priesthood.

The Government and the schools

Fig 13 Pademba Road, Freetown in 1856 showing Christ Church

In Britain in the early nineteenth century the Government did little for education. Schools were run by churches and private organizations. It was the same in the colonies, where the Government spent little on schools and left missions and churches to run them.

Almost every church in the Colony had a school attached to it. It was full of churches — and full of schools. But the churches were poor. In the villages particularly the congregations could not afford to give them much. So the schools were badly equipped and the teachers badly paid, indeed many teachers hardly earned enough to live on.

About the middle of the nineteenth century people in Britain discovered that there were not nearly enough schools for all the British children — thousands could not read or write. So the Government started giving money for education.

In Sierra Leone, too, it was felt that the Government should do more. In 1868 an inspector went round the schools and found conditions unsatisfactory. The teachers were doing their best, but they were discouraged by low pay and by lack of books and writing material. The government then began giving an annual grant for schools. But it was only a few hundred pounds a year among eighty or ninety schools, and when times were bad and revenue fell, no grant was given.

The Krio (Creole) community

The recaptives' children born in Sierra Leone were called 'Creoles'. This word 'Creole' came to be pronounced, and eventually written, 'Krio'.

By the 1870s many of the original recaptives had died. The Settlers had intermarried and merged into the Krio community. The old distinctions of 'Recaptive', 'Settler' and 'Krio' were blurred, and the name Krio may be applied to them all. People from the surrounding country who settled in the Colony and adopted its ways were also considered Krio.

Most of them aimed at attaining a European standard of life. They were Christians; they wore European clothes; they lived in houses of European style. But they were not just imitation Europeans. They had

Fig 14 Christian missionaries hated African religious ceremonies. Here a missionary is attacking an Egungun dancer in a Freetown street

their own Krio language, which was different from English. They kept old customs brought from their African homelands, particularly their music and dancing. They had their own companies and local government, organized without European help in their own way. Though some of the more highly educated among them despised these things, they still went on.

In East Freetown the Muslim Aku preserved their own identity (see pages 54–5). But they still felt themselves part of the Krio community, even though they retained their own religion and customs. Indeed some Yoruba customs, such as membership of the Egungun, or Oji, Society, were practised by both Christians and Muslims.

The recaptives, men of little education, were mostly traders or farmers. A wider field opened before their children. Two young men, James Africanus Horton and William Broughton Davies, were sent to England by the army authorities, studied medicine, qualified as doctors, and in 1859 entered the British army as medical officers. They served until 1881 when they each retired with the rank of lieutenant-colonel.

Others went privately to Europe to study medicine at their own, or their families', expense. Robert Smith, T. H. Spilsbury, Daniel Taylor and Michael Jarrett qualified as doctors and were taken on in government service in Sierra Leone or other British colonies. By 1885 thirteen had qualified.

The first qualified barrister was a Maroon descendant, John Thorpe, who was called to the English bar in 1850. He never returned to Freetown. The next were Francis Smith (Dr Robert Smith's brother), and the most famous of them all, Samuel Lewis.

The Parliamentary Committee of 1865 had recommended that Africans be encouraged to take over government (see pages 71–2). Increasingly therefore they were given official recognition. The Rev George Nicol was appointed Colonial Chaplain in the Gambia, the Rev Thomas Maxwell in the Gold Coast. Three more Africans, Syble Boyle and Henry Lumpkin, recaptive shopkeepers, and William Grant, were given seats on the Legislative Council.

William Grant was born in the Colony of Ibo parents. He grew up with little education, but he read widely and educated himself. He traded as Heddle's agent, then on his own, doing a large business in the Northern Rivers. Tall and dignified in appearance, he went his own way uninfluenced by popular prejudices, earning the name Independent Grant.

A man who had great influence over the Krio community at this time was William Rainy, an Afro-West-Indian barrister. He had strong views which he aired fearlessly in the courts and in the newspapers he owned. Much of what he said was just violent abuse of officials he disliked, but he showed the people how to expose official misdoings, and encouraged them to organize against the government when it ignored their views.

King Macaulay died in 1868, and Isaac Benjamin Pratt succeeded him as Aku king, but when Pratt died in 1880 the kingship came to an end. The community was forgetting its old divisions, and becoming a more united group. 'A *national* spirit is being developed', wrote Dr Africanus Horton.

In 1868 A. B. C. Sibthorpe, a village teacher, published the first History and Geography of Sierra Leone, showing the world that the country had an identity of its own and that its inhabitants were a distinctive people, proud of their achievements.

CHAPTER NINETEEN
Mende expansion

How the Mende expanded

By the nineteenth century the Mende were well established in the Sher-bro hinterland (see pages 59–60). They built large towns, each formed of a cluster of small towns, strongly stockaded with high fences. Inside

Fig 15 A Mende warfence

the fences the houses were built close together, connected by narrow passages, so that if enemies got in they would find it difficult to fight.

Each town had its own rulers. There was no king over all the Mende, but they recognized Taiama as their main town. Built on high ground on the banks of the River Taia, Taiama was made up of nine stockaded towns and seven open villages. It had nearly ten thousand inhabitants.

The chiefs who ruled these Mende strongholds had usually gained a reputation in war. As we have seen, they were often called in to fight in neighbouring wars, rewarded, if they were victorious, with a share of the captives and plundered goods.

But not all Mende lived by war. Most were farmers; some were traders. Groups of Mende would move into Bulom country to farm and trade. The Bulom rulers would let them settle down under their jurisdiction. More and more moved in until they outnumbered the Bulom inhabitants. Then they would elect their own headmen, and though still in name subject to a Bulom landlord, they would be virtually independent, and their towns Mende towns.

Richard Canre Ba Caulker became chief of the Bumpe country in 1864. He had been educated in Freetown at the Grammar School, and liked to compare himself with the Kings of England and of Israel whom he had learnt about. He was also a Poro member. But he could not control the Mende who moved into his country. Their chiefs, still in name his subjects, did as they chose. He could only keep them down by setting one against the other in a policy of 'divide and rule'.

Many Mende flocked into Bonthe, the government headquarters, seeking work. They were employed as labourers on the roads and other public works. Thus they spread over the whole country until even their language began to supersede Bulom.

The slave trade continues

The British Government imagined that, by preventing the export of slaves across the Atlantic, it had stopped the slave trade. But though the Atlantic trade had ceased, slaves were still bought and sold. There was increasing demand for vegetable produce (palm oil and kernels in the Sherbro country, groundnuts in the north) for the European market. Slaves were needed, to grow and harvest the produce, and as the market expanded, the demand for slaves increased. Kings and chiefs wanted as many slaves as possible, to provide them with produce to exchange for imported goods.

So wars were still fought in order to obtain slaves. But now the slaves were not exported overseas, to work for Europeans across the Atlantic. They were put to work in Africa, by African masters, to grow or harvest vegetable produce for export to Europe.

'British Sherbro'

The British Government did not want the expense of governing the land annexed in 1861. Administration was confined to the main centres — Bonthe, Bendu and York Island. A few policemen were also posted throughout the country. Otherwise the rulers continued as before. It was 'British Sherbro' only in name.

Slavery was not recognized by English law. It should therefore have been abolished in this supposedly British territory. But the Government did not have the means of abolishing it, and dared not antagonize the rulers by trying. All that was done was to say that any slave who escaped to a British town like Bonthe was free. Elsewhere, though slavery was not officially recognized, it was allowed to go on.

Trade in the Mende country

The European traders in the Sherbro were unenterprising. They built premises near the coast and stayed there (like the old slave-traders) waiting for trade. It was Krio traders who opened Mende country to trade. Many went in as petty traders, going round the villages with a small stock of goods, then, as they made money, building premises and employing agents.

Many Krio women went trading in this way. The Settler women had always traded (see page 35), and it was also an Aku tradition for women to trade, as they did at home in the Yoruba country.

A woman would often leave her husband and children for long periods and go off trading on her own. The Freetown or Bonthe shops would advance her goods on credit — looking-glasses, or coloured handkerchiefs, or scented soap — that would attract customers, and she would wander round the country selling them. Some women became rich and had stores built to keep goods in, and employed men as clerks and storekeepers.

Chiefs who had controlled trade in the slave-trading days, keeping a close watch on their stranger, knowing exactly how much he was making, now found they had lost control. There were Krio traders everywhere, competing fiercely with one another, cutting prices to undersell rivals, buying up produce before it was ripe to prevent rivals from getting it. The more enterprising chiefs realized that, as they could no longer control trade, they must trade themselves.

J. A. Williams was a prosperous Krio trader at Mafwe (near Sumbuya) on the Bum River. Unlike some traders who only worked selfishly for their own interests, he was ready to work for the public good. He often mediated in wars: the Government recognized his services by presenting him with a gold watch.

Fula, Susu and Mandinka traders also moved into the Sherbro country, to buy and sell slaves, which British traders were forbidden to do. Some grew rich. Unlike the British traders, they had no government to protect them. Sometimes Bulom and Mende rulers would turn against them, plunder them, and drive them penniless from the country.

Gbanya

Gbanya was a famous military leader in Kpa-Mende (the western part of Mende country). Even the British 'bought war' from him during the Koya War (see page 67). In 1873, when the British Government in the Gold Coast were fighting Asante, Gbanya sent a party of Mende to fight on the British side.

He extended his power over the Bulom towns in the Upper Bumpe River, and settled at Senehun, the Bumpe river-head, where produce from Taiama and the country round was brought to be shipped by canoe or sailing boat to Freetown. Many traders congregated there in their own town by the wharf, so he was not only famous in war but the ruler of a large trading-centre.

Christian missions

Some Krio traders held regular religious services in their houses or built churches. But these were for their own benefit. They were not mission churches.

But the missionary societies also had a few stations. The CMS. went back to Port Loko, and the Methodists went to the Mabanta and Limba countries. The Limba mission was for many years directed by the Rev P. P. Hazely, a Krio missionary, known as 'the apostle to the Limba'. But they made few converts.

By far the most successful missionaries were the Americans of the UBC and the Mendi Mission (which joined together). The Rev Joseph Gomer, an Afro-American at Shenge, converted Thomas Stephen Caulker, who died a Christian in 1871 after reigning forty years.

The American missionaries taught improved methods of farming. They built a saw-mill at Mano Bagru and taught their schoolboys how to work it. Thus they attracted boys who wanted to learn new skills. When boys left school and wanted to trade, the mission advanced them goods on credit, keeping a hold on their converts, who were encouraged to go round preaching as well as trading.

They also sent boys to the United States for education. Among them was Daniel Flickinger Wilberforce. His father lived in Bonthe; his mother was related to the ruling family of Imperi. He was ordained a minister of the UBC Church, returned with an American wife, and settled at Gbambaia, Imperi. A man of considerable learning, a fine preacher and a good musician, he was able through his family connexions to exert great influence in Imperi and the surrounding country.

In these ways the UBC rooted itself in the country.

Immigration into the Colony

Many Mende, Temne and Limba, dissatisfied with life in their own countries, sought work in Freetown where they were paid wages in cash, which they could not get at home. They were also out of their chiefs' power. Unused to getting wages, they were ready to work for less money than local labourers, and provided a cheap labour supply for employers.

Some Freetown people were suspicious of immigrants. They were afraid that, as more and more came in, they would introduce their own customs and undermine the existing way of life. So, unless the immigrants worked in households, they remained apart from the rest of the community, settling chiefly in eastern Freetown.

CHAPTER TWENTY

Scarcies to Mano

Extending the customs area

John Pope Hennessy was appointed temporary Governor in 1872. He was a man who wanted everyone to love him, and longed to be popular. When he heard that some of the poorer people found it a hardship to pay the House Tax he abolished taxes and increased customs duties instead.

The Colony's wealth depended on European trade: produce was exported from Freetown to Europe. If there was a demand for it the Colony prospered; if not, the Colony suffered. Soon after Hennessy left, trade was depressed all over Europe, and there was little market for African produce. Imports and exports declined, so there was less money from customs revenue. Soon there was not enough money to pay for the government.

It was proposed to restore the House Tax, but the people would not hear of it. They loved Hennessy for having abolished it; they celebrated August 22nd, the day he abolished it, 'Pope Hennessy Day', as an annual holiday. In the face of their opposition the Government dared not restore it. Instead customs duties were increased still higher.

Traders disliked having to pay these heavy customs duties (see page 71). If, instead of trading in Freetown, they traded from premises on the rivers, beyond the government's reach, they did not need to pay them. They began moving away to the rivers, where they could sell unduticd imported goods for less than the dutied goods in Freetown. This attracted customers. Freetown shopkeepers were alarmed, fearing that they were going to lose all their trade.

William Grant put before the Colonial Office a plan to restore Freetown's prosperity. He proposed that the coastline to the north and south be annexed. In this way the traders in the neighbourhood would be brought under British rule and obliged to pay customs.

Grant and his Krio countrymen disliked feeling they belonged only to a small colony and that once they were across its borders they were in foreign territory. They wanted the areas where they traded brought under English law, and wanted the Government to stop wars there. So his plan was popular in Freetown, for it seemed the first step to the creation of a large colony.

The British Government was still unwilling to annex any more of West Africa, but it also insisted that colonies must pay for themselves. Each colony had to raise enough money out of customs or taxes to pay its own expenses. It looked as if the Colony of Sierra Leone could only pay its way if its customs area was extended.

So the Government was told to make treaties with the neighbouring chiefs which would bring their countries under control of the customs. But in no other way was the area to be British. No money was to be spent protecting or developing it. This mean policy was merely devised to collect money without undertaking any new responsibility, and could not satisfy Grant's hopes.

The Northern Rivers

Some still hoped that the customs area might be extended over the Northern Rivers as far as the Rio Nunez. The chiefs there had made treaties of friendship long before (see page 56). But since then the French had stepped in (see page 72), and there was a French post at the mouth of the Melakori blocking the way northward.

The Scarcies chiefs made treaties which put their countries under the Freetown customs, but the French Government would not allow any customs treaties beyond. In 1882 the British and French Governments agreed that the Scarcies and the rivers south of it should be British, the Melakori and the rivers north of it French. The rulers of the rivers were not consulted. The Temne, Susu and other peoples who lived in the area were now divided from one another by a frontier fixed in Europe.

This gave the groundnut trade to the French. They built up Conakry from a village into a big port where groundnuts could be shipped to France. By the end of the 1880s almost no groundnuts were exported from Freetown.

Some Krio traders suffered from being brought under an unsympathetic French Government, but many stayed and went on trading in the Northern Rivers. Frenchmen traded in Sierra Leone too. One of the biggest firms was 'French Company' founded by a French trader, C. A. Verminck.

John Caulker's War

Shortly before Thomas Stephen Caulker of Shenge died, the Caulker family were summoned to Freetown to decide who should succeed him. His son George Stephen was fixed on. But some of the family disapproved of the choice, and when he succeeded there were several attempts to remove him.

Among the discontented was John Caulker, the chief's cousin and Speaker. They quarrelled violently, and John 'bought war' from Gbanya and attacked him (see page 82). The war swept through the whole Bagru country, including the British part. A British officer went over from Bonthe to complain and was driven away badly wounded.

Dr Samuel Rowe was Governor at this time. He was an army doctor who had spent many years in West Africa. Most governors stayed in Freetown, but Rowe was an energetic man who got bored if he had to sit still. He loved to get out of Freetown and go travelling through the bush. The Mende called him 'Old Red Breeches' because he went so fast he seemed to have fire in his trousers. He always took his office

Fig 16 A meeting between the Bulom Shore chiefs and Governor Rowe. Rowe sits on the chair, T. G. Lawson stands beside him

staff with him, and at the end of a hard day's walking, would sit down happily and dictate letters to the Colonial Office, telling them what he was doing. The clerks who had to write the letters, and put up with his bad temper if anything went wrong, did not care much for these expeditions.

Rowe at once took a force of soldiers and police to the Bagru country to punish those who had invaded British territory. He went up the river, and then by land through Kpa-Mende country. The people were amazed to see him: no Colony official had ever been there before. He summoned Gbanya and asked why he had allowed his men to make war in British territory. Gbanya could find no answer, so Rowe had him flogged. This was a great humiliation for a powerful chief like Gbanya.

No one felt like fighting a fierce governor of this kind. Gbanya and the other Mende chiefs promised not to make war again. John Caulker and his two leading followers were given up. They were tried for murder committed on British soil, and hanged at Bendu.

In addition the two Caulker chiefs agreed to let the Government collect customs in their countries. This extended the customs area over the coast between the Colony peninsula and British Sherbro.

John Myer Harris of Sulima

John Myer Harris, a Jewish trader, arrived in the Sherbro to trade about 1855. After a few years he began taking ships to the Gallinas estuary. All this part of the country was owned by the Liberian Government, which had made treaties there with the chiefs (see page 62). They said he must pay them customs duties, but he refused.

The Government backed Harris up, for British traders did not want to have to pay Liberian customs. Harris said the chiefs had never given their country to Liberia, and had only made treaties of friendship. He made friends with the chief of Jurung who let him build a large trading establishment at Sulima at the mouth of the Moa. There he settled, trading in produce, without paying customs either to Liberia or the British.

The Liberians complained to the British Government in London, who suggested that they send a Commission to ask the chiefs whether or not they had given up their country. The Liberians refused to agree, fearing that Harris would bribe the chiefs to say they had not given it up.

So things remained as they were. Harris remained at Sulima, married into his landlord's family, and became a Poro member — probably one of the first Europeans to join.

The Liberian frontier

On several occasions Liberian forces went to the Mano River to make the British traders respect Liberian sovereignty. The traders complained to the Freetown government that they had been plundered and demanded compensation. But the Liberians were too poor to pay.

Edward Wilmot Blyden was a distinguished Liberian citizen. Born in the West Indies of African descent, he migrated to Liberia. A brilliant scholar who could speak several languages, with a fertile mind full of original ideas, he made many influential friends in England and the United States. Several American universities conferred the degree of doctor on him. He travelled much, and often visited Freetown.

In 1877 he went to London on behalf of the Liberian Government to try to settle who owned the disputed territory. The British Government, now seeking to extend the customs area, were interested. They wanted to fix a definite frontier with Liberia so that all traders would have to pay customs to one or the other. A Boundary Commission was sent to investigate, but could reach no agreement.

The British Government was impatient for a speedy settlement. In 1882 Governor Havelock, Rowe's successor, went to Monrovia with a naval escort to offer the Liberian Government the following terms — they must give up all claim to the disputed territory, and the British would give up all claim to compensation for the plundered traders. Vainly the Liberians protested against such an unfair bargain. They were powerless. They had against them the might of the British Empire, the most powerful empire in the world. Eventually in 1886 they signed a treaty giving up their territory, and fixing the coastal frontier at the Mano River.

Meanwhile the Governor had made treaties with all the coastal rulers, allowing the British authorities to collect customs duties in their countries, until the customs area stretched along the coast from Scarcies to Mano.

CHAPTER TWENTY-ONE

The Trade Wars of the 1880s

Produce-trading chiefs

As trade increased in the Sherbro hinterland, wars broke out more often. Rival chiefs contested the ownership of the trading centres, or tried to divert trade from their rivals' countries to their own. The captives taken in battle were employed as slaves to enrich the victors.

Enterprising traders gained power at the expense of rulers who did not trade (as in the eighteenth century) (see pages 19–20). During the nineteenth century (and perhaps earlier) Krim was ruled by a succession of ladies with the title Queen Messe. By the late 1870s Queen Messe and her neighbour Zorokong, who ruled the adjoining chiefdom to the south, were overshadowed by Fawundu of Mano on Kasse Lake.

Fig 17 Momo Ja and Momo Kai Kai with their retinue

Subject in name to Zorokong, he grew rich through trade, built a large town and dominated the country.

The country round Pujehun (or Gombu), the river-head of the Wanje, a tributary of the Kittam, also belonged to Zorokong. But it passed under the control of Momo Ja and Momo Kai Kai. They were the sons of Fula fathers and Mende mothers who, like Fawundu, grew rich through trade. Pujehun became the centre for all the produce brought from the country round. They kept out rivals and worked to gain control of all the Kittam trade.

When wars broke out, traders would take sides, calling on the British Government for help. Traders who chose to live beyond the frontier were not supposed to have official protection, but government officers would sometimes intervene, often without understanding the causes of the war, to try to make peace, usually by supporting one side against the other in a dispute.

Europeans often called these wars 'tribal wars', as if to suggest that Africans had no serious motives for fighting, and that one 'tribe' was always fighting another for no reason. But this was not so. The combattants in these wars had a serious economic objective — the control of trade. Nor were they necessarily aligned by 'tribes'. (See page 3). Political boundaries cut across speech boundaries. Mende often fought against Mende, Temne against Temne.

S.B.A. Macfoy—'Sherbro Monarch'

One day some people were passing along the north shore of Sherbro Island in a canoe. A boy from Kent village, Solomon Benjamin Augustus Macfoy, was on board. When they reached Jamaica Point, the north-east tip of the island, they threw him out. He swam ashore safely and vowed that he would stay there and make his fortune.

Within twenty years he had fulfilled his vow. He had large premises at Jamaica and agents all over the country trading for him. Small and unimpressive-looking, with little education, he nevertheless commanded respect and fear. He worked hard himself, made others work hard for him, and allowed nothing to stand between him and what he wanted. Rivals were pushed out. He extended his business continually, buying up trading establishments everywhere. He understood the power of the new trading chiefs, and did business with Momo Ja and Momo Kai Kai, who used their influence for his interests.

He was agent for a Manchester firm which sent him £40 000 worth of goods every year. In return he sent produce, shipped in steamships which he hired specially from Europe. He also bought a steamship of his own, calling it by his nickname 'Sherbro Monarch'.

Like most Krio traders, Macfoy wanted to see the whole trading area annexed and put under English law. He was impatient with the Government which did nothing to stop wars. In England he had influential business friends. Through them he got the Colonial Office to send back Rowe, a strong Governor, who Macfoy hoped would bring the country under British rule.

But Rowe came back with strict orders from the Colonial Office not to annex any more territory. All he could do was travel about, visiting areas where war threatened and telling the people not to fight.

But they were no longer afraid of Rowe. While he was with them they promised peace; once he was gone they prepared for war again. All his exertions and journeys through the bush were for nothing, and Macfoy and the traders were no nearer annexation than they had been before.

Yoni Wars

The Yoni still wanted their share of the Rokel trade (see page 65). All through the 1870s they kept on fighting Masimera and Marampa. Magbele, their objective, was reduced from a town of five or six thousand inhabitants to a village of three or four huts.

But the Rokel was no longer the important trading area it had been. Timber was no longer exported, and traders now congregated further south near the Mende palm forests. Rather than go on fighting to gain a place that was now of little value, the Yoni changed their policy. In 1883 they made peace with Masimera and Marampa, gave up trying to get a trading centre on the Rokel and determined to get one on the Ribi or Bumpe River instead.

The nearest big centre for them to attack was Rotifunk on the Bumpe River, ruled by a Loko chief, Suri Kesebe, whom the Caulkers had allowed to settle there after the Temne-Loko War. He had become an important chief, and Richard Caulker was jealous of him. It was believed Caulker was secretly helping the Yoni against him.

Rotifunk was well fortified. As well as his own Loko followers, Suri had about two hundred Fula traders living there, and was also given help by the British Government. So the Yoni failed to get it.

Next they turned to Koya. A group of them raided the Koya Loko at Songo Town. Whether they knew it or not, Songo Town was in the Colony. Several people living there were carried away as slaves.

Everyone in the Colony was enraged at this invasion of British territory.

Rowe hurried out to Koya, then entered Yoni country, but the raiders withdrew inland and he had to return to Freetown without being able to punish them.

Trade again depressed

During the mid-1880s there was another period when trade in Europe was depressed. The price of palm oil and kernels fell. Although more palm produce was being gathered than ever before to be exported to Europe, the low prices it was fetching made traders unwilling to buy. Freetown trade, which depended on exports, suffered again as it had in the early 1870s.

Once again Freetown people demanded that the surrounding country be annexed. They said that the real cause of the trade depression was the many wars in the interior. They believed that if the trading area could only be brought under British rule, and wars put down, trade would revive. In fact there was plenty of produce being gathered. It was the low prices, not wars, that prevented them making a profit. But they wanted annexation and were as ready to use bad reasons as good to get their way.

Again the British Government refused to hear of it. If territory was annexed it brought added expense. There would have to be officials and police in the annexed area; government buildings and roads would have to be built. The Colony could not afford to pay for them — and the British would not.

The trade depression also affected the trading chiefs who brought produce for sale and found prices were down. This annoyed them and made them readier to go to war.

Bokari Gomna and Makaia

Prince Mana of Gendema died in 1872. His successor Jaia was old and blind. The power of the Massaquoi had greatly declined since the end of the slave trade, and Jaia could not rule his country properly. Bokari Gomna (or Governor), of part Mende, part Vai descent, determined to supplant him. In alliance with some inland Mende chiefs he seized the Massaquoi crown, a large silver crown. He is also believed to have murdered Jaia.

Macfoy went to make peace. He brought powerful medicines and made the contestants swear to stop fighting. He then made friends with

Bokari, and offered him £100 credit to start trading. The coastal chiefs, including Fawundu, were alarmed, fearing that if Bokari had Macfoy behind him he would soon control trade in the whole Gallinas country. They started a special Poro, pretending it was only to rebuild Gendama, which had been destroyed in war. Really they swore that they would destroy Bokari.

About sixty kilometres inland lived Makaia, who had grown famous in war, then turned to trade. Bokari's enemies asked him to help them and he invaded the coastal area. Some of his men attacked Sulima, where the British customs station was, but were beaten off by the police. He then retired inland, where he began diverting trade away from Sulima, making people take their produce along the Kittam River instead. Bokari eventually took refuge in Freetown.

The Government was angry with Makaia for attacking Sulima. He replied that his men were not to blame, for there was no sign to show where the British zone started. He also explained that he was no enemy to the British, indeed that he was anxious to go on trading with them.

Macfoy took up farming during the trade depression, and laid out large plantations at Jamaica. On the mainland he forced chiefs who owed him money to give him their land. In this way he controlled much of Imperi, where he planted in his usual ruthless style, breaking down villages that stood in his way. But his agricultural plans were cut short by his death in 1893.

Samori

During the 1870s Samori, a Muslim Mandinka, rose to power in the Upper Niger country. He built up an army of soldiers called the Sofas. When two chiefs were at war, he would intervene and take the defeated chief's country as his own. When he took a town, the men were told to become Muslims and join his army. If they refused, he killed them. The Sofas fought savagely, suddenly appearing on horseback to surprise their enemies. Wherever they went they left a trail of burning towns behind them.

King Sewa of Falaba quarrelled with the neighbouring chief of Kaliere, who called in the Sofas. Falaba was a strongly fortified town. Its inhabitants had always resisted Islam and were determined not to yield to Samori or accept his religion (see page 16). There was a long siege. The Sofas surrounded Falaba, and though they could not take it, they prevented food getting in.

Soon Sewa and his people were starving. Still they would not submit.

Fig 18 Mounted Sofa warrior

Sewa called his leading men to a large store filled with barrels of gunpowder and asked if any of them were ready to give in to Samori and
Islam. All refused. Then he seized a lighted torch, threw it into the
gunpowder, and blew himself and them up, preferring suicide to the
humiliation of surrender.

Samori bought the arms he fought with in Freetown, where Sofa
caravans went regularly, so he advanced from Falaba into Limba country
to be nearer his arms supply. The Temne feared they would be his next
victims.

Meanwhile the French were advancing eastwards from Senegal into the
countries Samori was conquering. He realized that sooner or later he
would have to fight them. It was important for him to remain friendly
with the British and be sure of getting arms to fight with. When Rowe
sent a message asking him not to invade Temne country, he promised
he would not.

Thus beyond Temne and Mende country the interior was being
occupied by one of two invaders — Samori or the French.

CHAPTER TWENTY-TWO
Preparing for self-government

Hopes for the future

Since 1865 the peoples of British West Africa had been able to look
forward to the day when the British would withdraw and leave them to
govern themselves (see pages 71–2). Freetown people felt increasingly
that with their educational achievements, and their experience in senior
official posts, they would soon be ready for self-government.

Fig 19 The teachers and pupils of Charlotte School in the 1880s

Higher education

Partly at William Grant's suggestion, the CMS agreed in 1876 to
affiliate Fourah Bay College to Durham University in England. This

enabled the students to study for English university degrees. Durham University sent out examination papers and awarded degrees to those who passed them. The first were awarded in 1879.

The curriculum only included arts subjects and theology. Those who wanted to qualify as doctors and barristers still had to go to Europe. J. F. Easmon, a Settler descendant, qualified as a doctor in London and Brussels (Belgium), and was appointed to the government service in the Gold Coast (Ghana), where he rose to be head of the medical department. He did research into malaria and was the first to isolate blackwater fever as a separate disease, one of the first original contributions made by an African doctor to European medical science.

Among those who were called to the bar at this time were J.A.M' Carthy and A. S. Hebron. Both were the sons of rich Freetown shopkeepers who could afford to send their sons to be expensively educated in England. M'Carthy was appointed Queen's Advocate in 1890. This post (later called Attorney-General) made him legal adviser to the Government with a seat on the Executive Council.

Fig 20 Sir Samuel Lewis

Samuel Lewis

Samuel Lewis was the most famous barrister. He had a deep knowledge of law and worked unceasingly — often starting work at three or four in the morning. When he took up a case he devoted all his energies to winning it, and was usually successful. He was offered government posts but refused them. He preferred to keep his independence and say what he felt without being tied to the government.

He also ignored popular prejudices, making himself many enemies in Freetown, but still not swerving from saying and doing what he thought was right.

Though he would not accept government employment, he served his people on the Legislative Council, to which he was appointed in 1882 after William Grant died. He criticized the Government fearlessly when he thought it was wrong, but helped it when he thought it was right. When a Freetown Municipality was introduced in 1895 he was chosen mayor, and given a British title of distinction, a knighthood, making him Sir Samuel Lewis.

Dr Blyden in Freetown

Dr Blyden often visited Freetown at this time (see page 88). People felt proud to welcome this distinguished scholar. He wrote articles for the two best Freetown newspapers — William Grant's *West African Reporter*, which was published from 1876 to 1884, and the *Sierra Leone Weekly News*, owned and edited by Cornelius May, published from 1886 to 1951.

Dr Blyden had wide views which embraced all Africa, indeed he was one of the originators of the 'Pan-Africanism' that developed in the twentieth century. He was also interested in Islam. Once, on a visit to Egypt, a Muslim country, he suddenly realized how Islam united Africans right across the continent. He made friends with the Freetown Muslims. When the government began giving money to Muslim schools he did all he could to encourage them, and for a while held the post of Director of Muslim Education.

Farming

In Freetown those who made money usually made it out of trade. Farming did not bring large profits. Some people farmed in the villages

97

Fig 21 Dr Edward Blyden

and sold their produce in Freetown. In the 1860s many of them took to growing ginger for export. But they did not know how to prepare it properly for export and never got a very good price. Prices varied continually. One year there might be a demand for ginger in Europe and the price would be quite high; next year there would be more for sale than was wanted, and the price would fall. The farmers became discouraged, and stopped growing ginger for export.

Nor did large scale plantations succeed. William Grant and Sir Samuel Lewis both bought land and laid out large plantations, but neither succeeded in making them pay.

A nation of shopkeepers

The English were once called 'a nation of shopkeepers'. The phrase might well be applied to the Krio community in the nineteenth century. Apart from those who entered the professions, almost all who prospered did so by importing and exporting, as their recaptive fathers had done.

Take Malamah Thomas. He grew up, a poor boy, in Hastings village,

Fig 22 Freetown Post Office. From 1828 to 1835 it was the Governor's house (photograph taken in 1870)

Fig 23 Central Freetown in the 1890s, a photograph taken from the Cathedral tower looking south and showing the mansions owned by wealthy citizens. The four-storey house on the left is Horton Hall, home of Dr Africanus Horton

going straight out to work on his father's farm as soon as school was over. At fourteen he became a trader's clerk in the Northern Rivers. He saved his earnings and started trading on his own at Malamah (which he adopted às his name) on the Sierra Leone River. He had a shop in Freetown, too, which his wife managed when he was away. He enlarged his Freetown business, specializing in imported cottons, and patented his own variety, 'Malamah Baft', which became famous.

Tall and majestic in appearance, he did things on a grand scale. He built a large house in Little East Street ornamented with carved heads. He gave generously to the poor. When his daughter married, he hired half the houses in the street to entertain the guests, and the whole city shared in the lavish wedding festivities.

For a contrast compare him with Abukeh Thomas (though they had the same surname the two Thomases were not related). He too grew up in a village, Wellington. He moved to Freetown as a shopkeeper, starting with the small capital his father had made by farming. Gradually he became rich. But where Malamah was generous, Abukeh was miserly. He lived like a poor man. He and his wife ate the cheapest food. He invested his profits in England, where no one in Freetown could know about them. People guessed he must be rich, but he never admitted it, and was angry if anyone suggested it. When he died, he was worth over £70 000 which he left to found an Agricultural College at Mabang.

Those who were in business elsewhere in West Africa prospered too. R. B. Blaize, born in Freetown, became one of the richest men in Lagos. Horton Jones, from Gloucester village, became one of the richest in the Gambia. Maximiliano Jones, from Waterloo, became a rich planter in Fernando Po. Traders and professional men who settled in Accra or Lagos bought up land and houses, basing their prosperity on house-property and rents as the Settlers and recaptives had in Freetown.

Governor MacCarthy's dream come true

Governor MacCarthy's dream had come true (see pages 40–1). He had dreamed of training up a people who would spread the ideals he cherished — Christianity and European education. This had happened. Churches and schools in all the British West African colonies depended on missionaries and teachers from Sierra Leone. The government services depended on officials — including doctors, magistrates, and senior administrative officers — from Sierra Leone. All along the West African coast they were to be found. They were the intellectual leaders, the vanguard of political and social advance in West Africa.

CHAPTER TWENTY-THREE

The end of the Trade Wars

Madam Yoko

Madam Yoko was the head wife of Chief Gbanya of Senehun (see pages 82, 86–7). She was a woman of commanding appearance and a fine dancer. She was a member of the Sande Society, and girls from all over Mende country were attracted to her Sande Bush where they received the best training available.

Gbanya died in 1878, and after his death his country passed increasingly under her influence. It is said that when Gbanya was dying he asked Rowe to recognize her as his successor. This Rowe did. She moved to Senehun, the most important town in her chiefdom.

Madam Yoko had statesmanlike powers of persuasion. All European officials who visited her were impressed by her, and she usually succeeded in getting them to do what she wanted. If a rival chief threatened her, she would tell the Governor that she was a poor defenceless woman menaced by a dangerous enemy — and he would send her help. Policemen were stationed at Senehun to protect her. In this way she became immensely powerful.

William Caulker's War

George Stephen Caulker of Shenge fell ill in 1881, came to Freetown and was operated on, but died. His half-brother Thomas Neale Caulker came with him. He was an intelligent man with some education, and the Government recognized him as successor.

This enraged many of the Caulker family. Thomas Neale's mother was a slave-woman and they felt he had no right to be chief. Among his opponents was William Caulker, an old enemy of the late chief's. He and some of his relatives resolved to get rid of Thomas Neale. They 'bought war' from the Mende, and in 1887 suddenly invaded Shenge chiefdom, destroying towns, killing and enslaving with great ferocity, advancing on Shenge.

The Rev D. F. Wilberforce had just moved to Shenge to be principal of a training school the UBC were building there. William Caulker had a grudge against the mission people and had sworn to destroy the mission. But Wilberforce brought in men of his own from Imperi, his mother's country, to defend it. There was a fierce struggle and William's men were driven off. A British gunboat then anchored off Shenge; police landed, and the invaders scattered. William and his associates were arrested and brought to Freetown. After a trial lasting nearly five months he and two others were hanged at Shenge.

People in Freetown had great sympathy for William (who had given his men orders to kill no Krio) and were angry at his being hanged. They said that if the British Government had taken its responsibilities seriously and brought Shenge under its rule intead of just greedily exacting customs duties, the war would never have taken place. William seemed to them a victim of British policy, and his war another argument in favour of annexing the neighbouring countries.

The Yoni Expedition

The Yoni were still fighting for a trading-centre near the Bumpe River. The Mende there retaliated and invaded Yoni country. Vainly the British Government tried to mediate between them. The war spread, and a party of Mende invaded British Koya.

In 1887 some Yoni attacked Senehun. Madam Yoko was away but several Krio traders were killed. When the news reached the Colonial Office, it was decided to send a military expedition to stop these wars. As the Yoni were the most recent aggressors the expedition was against them.

Two hundred soldiers marched out from Freetown, joined by seven hundred allies, chiefly Mende and Loko, who took advantage of the expedition to retaliate on Yoni. Rockets were fired at Robari, a stockaded town on the edge of Yoni country, and the defenders retreated inland. A garrison of soldiers was then stationed at Robari to prevent further invasion.

So Yoni hopes of winning a trading-centre were frustrated.

The war against Makaia

Meanwhile Makaia was still diverting trade from Sulima to the Kittam River (see page 93). But he quarrelled with Momo Kai Kai, who controlled much of the Kittam trade.

A British officer, Captain Crawford, was sent to Sulima in charge of the customs post. About fifty policemen were stationed there to protect it. Crawford had strict orders not to fight unless attacked. But he was ambitious, anxious to win glory in war, and wanted to punish Makaia for having raided Sulima. He made friends with Momo Ja and Momo Kai Kai, who were delighted to help him against their new enemy Makaia. Together they marched inland, captured his strongholds, and destroyed them. Makaia took refuge inland with Chief Nyagua of Panguma.

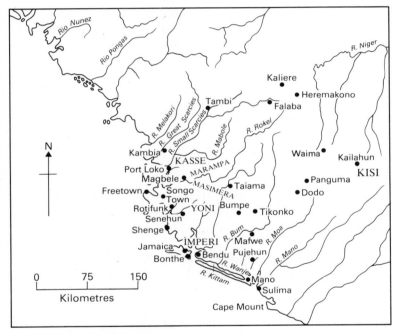

Map 4 The Era of the Trade Wars

Though Crawford had disobeyed orders in fighting a war, the British Government was delighted. Trade was freed and Sulima no longer menaced.

Nyagua of Panguma

Nyagua was the son of Faba, a famous military leader, who had built up a chiefdom round Dodo. Like many other chiefs he wanted to trade, but his route to the coast was blocked by a large encampment at Wende, where men flocked from all over the country and prevented trade passing. From Wende they went out raiding — plundering towns and enslaving the inhabitants.

In 1889 a government officer with some police, accompanied by Momo Ja and his followers, went to visit Nyagua. They broke up the thirteen stockaded towns that comprised Wende, where three thousand people were held as slaves, thus freeing the trade route to the interior. Nyagua, out of gratitude, then gave up Makaia.

Makaia was taken to Freetown and deported to the Gold Coast. Several chiefs who made war at this period were similarly deported to other British colonies — while chiefs who made war there were deported to Freetown. Every time anyone was deported, a special law had to be passed to make the deportation legal.

After Makaia was deported and Wende destroyed, Mendegla of Juru inaugurated a peace Poro which brought the wars to an end. Where the British Government had failed to bring peace, Poro succeeded.

New states

One result of the trade wars was that many small political units were amalgamated by powerful leaders into large states. Madam Yoko steadily increased her power in Kpa-Mende. Elsewhere others were doing the same.

The country round the upper part of the Moa and Mano Rivers was peopled by many small communities, Kisi and Mende, living peaceably together. But, as trade and warfare spread, a bitter war broke out there between two rivals, Kai Lundu and Ndawa. In about 1880 Kai Lundu was victorious, and united the whole country under his own rule in a new, large state, Luawa. He built Kailahun as his main town. Although he was very famous in war he was also kind and gentle in manner and merciful to his enemies.

East of Luawa, Nyagua was building up his own state, Panguma. Further south, Mendegla was doing the same, as were Momo Ja and Kai Kai at Pujehun.

It was the same in other parts of the country. In the north, among the Limba, where wealth was spread by traders coming from inland to the coast, Suluku of Bumban built up a large state. Everywhere small units of government were being consolidated into large states.

Fig 24 Kai Lundu of Luawa

CHAPTER TWENTY-FOUR
The European partition

Europe and Africa

Until the last quarter of the nineteenth century there were few European colonies in Africa. Most of the continent was ruled by African governments.

But from the late 1870s the governments of Europe began seizing territory from African rulers, until by about 1900 almost the whole continent was under their rule. Sometimes land was taken by conquest, sometimes by treaty. Often African rulers signed treaties without understanding them (see pages 23, 31, 45, 67). But Europeans paid little attention to African opinion.

Nor did they necessarily respect existing frontiers. They fixed the frontiers of their new possessions themselves, as it suited them (see page 85). All over Africa people found themselves cut off from their countryfolk and neighbours by lines drawn on maps in Europe — lines which were eventually to harden into permanent frontiers which have survived the departure of the Europeans who devised them.

British policy in Sierra Leone now became more aggressive. Instead of talking about withdrawing from West Africa (see pages 71–2), the British Government began to extend its influence inland.

New British policy

European naval ships were now worked by steam, not sails. They could go much faster and were not dependent on the wind, but instead were dependent on coal. They had to be regularly supplied with coal to heat the boilers which provided the steam. Freetown was the only British port in West Africa with a harbour suited for a naval coaling depot. So the British Government, which in the past had never taken much interest in Sierra Leone, now found it of great importance. Fortifications were built to protect the harbour and coaling depot.

The French were steadily advancing in the interior. Only Samori stood between them and the coastal plain. If they defeated him, there was nothing to prevent them from advancing into Mende and Temne country and confining the British to a narrow strip of coast. The British Government was afraid that if there was war with France the naval coaling depot would be captured, and the British navy, unable to get coal, would be driven from West Africa.

It was also feared that if the French hemmed them into such a narrow strip, they would take all the trade away from Freetown.

In 1890 a new policy was begun. The Governor was told to make treaties of friendship with as many chiefs as possible in the neighbouring countries. These treaties contained a promise not to make a treaty with any other European government. Thus the chiefs who made them were prevented from making treaties with the French, and the area of British influence was enlarged.

Two Commissioners were appointed to make treaties — G. H. Garrett and T. J. Alldridge. They visited many places where no European had been before. Alldridge later described his experiences in a book, *The Sherbro and Its Hinterland*, which includes interesting photographs and descriptions of Mende country at that time. He made treaties with Nyagua and Kai Lundu who welcomed friendship with the British.

The Frontier Police

Governor Hay, who succeeded Rowe, wanted to make sure that peace lasted. He travelled round persuading chiefs to cut roads and link their towns with their neighbours' towns. In this way a large area, covering the coastal plain, was opened up to British influence.

When the British intervened in wars, unless soldiers were sent (as in the Yoni Expedition), the fighting was done by policemen. A policemen might be on duty one day in the Freetown streets, and the next day be marching off to fight. Hay divided the police. Some were permanently assigned to police duties. The rest were formed into a new military Frontier Police.

The Frontier Police had European officers and Krio sub-officers. Some of the men ('Frontiers', they were called) were Krio. But as they were to be stationed up-country the Government also recruited up-country, if only to get men who would understand the language in the place they were posted to. Eventually most were non-Krio.

The Frontiers were armed with rifles, and wore a simple uniform — blue serge tunic and trousers and a red fez — to enable them to move easily through the bush without being hampered by the elaborate dress then worn by soldiers.

Fig 25 Frontier Police outside the blockhouse at Bandajuma

Frontiers were stationed in small groups in towns all through the protected area — that is, the area where the roads were cut. They had strict orders not to interfere with the chiefs' government; their duty was to see that no more wars broke out. They were also told not to interfere with local customs. So though the protected area was brought under British influence, it was not brought under English law, and domestic slavery was allowed to go on.

The chiefs did not object to this arrangement. They imagined that the Frontiers would be there to help them and were pleased to have them.

J. C. E. Parkes

When Lawson, the Government Interpreter, retired in 1888, he was succeeded by his assistant J. C. E. Parkes. Parkes was a Krio government clerk who had studied affairs in the neighbouring countries and gained an unrivalled knowledge of them. He had also learnt much from Lawson. In recognition of his importance he was made head of a special Department of Native Affairs, with the title Secretary of Native Affairs.

It has been said that the chiefs never trusted the Krio. This was not true of Parkes. They liked and respected him and had confidence in him.

Bai Bureh

During the 1880s there was a war of succession in the Melakori country. Kebalai, a military leader of Loko descent, was called in to fight. He was a remarkable organizer who gathered his followers from far afield over Temne, Limba and Mende countries. Many stories are told of his strength and courage. Once, they say, some men attacked him when he was defenceless, without arms. Seizing the nearest man by the ankle he used him as a weapon, struck down his assailants with him and drove them off.

For his prowess in war he was elected chief of Kasse, Small Scarcies, with the title Bai Bureh. His chiefdom was in treaty with the British; he received a stipend and sometimes let the Governor arbitrate in disputes with his neighbours.

War broke out in the Scarcies between Karimu of Samaia, and the Loko and Limba. Bai Bureh was called in against Karimu. As the fighting was within the protected area, Commissioner Garrett went and persuaded the Loko and Limba to stop fighting. Bai Bureh was enraged at their making peace without consulting him, and complained angrily. Garrett then arrested him in order to bring him to Freetown. As they went through Kasse, Bai Bureh stepped into the doorway of a house and escaped. Garrett had only a few Frontiers with him and dared not try to retake him.

Fighting went on (though Bai Bureh took no further part), and Frontiers were sent to stop it. They marched to Tambi, high up the Small Scarcies, where there was a stockaded stronghold. They attacked it and were driven away. Next year a larger force of Frontiers was sent to take it, but again they were defeated.

Now the Government swallowed its pride and called on Bai Bureh for help. He and his men accompanied the third expedition, which included a large force of soldiers. This time Tambi was taken easily. The British officers noted how Bai Bureh's men fought under strict discipline, obedient to his orders. Few war-chiefs could control their armies in this way.

The Sofa Expedition

Samori found the French too strong for him. They made him sign treaties putting his conquests under their protection, and told him to stop trading with Freetown. But as this meant giving up his arms supply, he refused, repudiated the treaties and offered his conquests to the

British instead. Governor Hay wanted to accept. But the British Government did not, fearing it would lead to war with France.

To prevent further disputes, the British and French Governments arranged to divide the whole country into two spheres. The French sphere would lie north of the Scarcies and include the land round the source of the Niger. The British would have the rest. This division was made without consulting, or even informing, the inhabitants.

In the British sphere, near Falaba, was a large Sofa war base, Heremakono. The French objected to hostile Sofas being allowed to encamp in their sphere, so the British Government persuaded them to leave. The French then occupied Heremakono themselves, ignoring British protests. They said that although it was in the British sphere they must occupy it to prevent the Sofas returning.

By taking Heremakono the French cut the Sofas' trade route to Freetown. So a party of Sofas advanced, with their usual slaughter, into Kono to open a new route. But the British, now in agreement with the French, no longer wanted to trade with them. In 1893 a large force, soldiers and Frontiers, left Freetown to drive them from the British sphere. They went by sea to Bendu, then marched to Panguma and on northwards into Kono, where they encamped at Waima.

There was a small party of French soldiers in Kono under a young officer, Lieutenant Maritz, who had come from the north. He made friends with Kurua Wara, one of Kai Lundu's and Nyagua's rivals. Kurua Wara had until then been friendly with the Sofas. Now he hoped for French support against his two enemies.

Maritz had not heard of the British expedition. When Kurua Wara told him that an army was encamped at Waima he supposed they were Sofas, and hurried to attack them in the early morning before dawn. When his men started firing the British fired back. Each side supposed the others were Sofas. Ten British and eleven French, including Maritz, were killed before they discovered their mistake.

After this, a force of Frontiers under a Krio sub-officer, Charles Taylor, discovered the main body of the Sofas and defeated them, while the soldiers attacked the rest and drove them from the British sphere.

The French blamed Kurua Wara for not having warned Maritz about the British expedition, and held him responsible for the deaths at Waima. To punish him, a French officer had him beheaded. Once he was dead, Nyagua and Kai Lundu invaded his country and extended their territory over it.

Samori meanwhile, driven east by the French, moved eight hundred kilometres eastwards with all his people, numbering about 100 000, and founded a new state in the northern part of what is now Ghana — an

110

amazing feat of organization. But the inexorable French advance over inland West Africa eventually caught up with him, driving him southwest into the forests of Ivory Coast. There he was captured in 1898, and sent into exile where he died.

CHAPTER TWENTY-FIVE
The *Protectorate*

Planning a Protectorate

The British and French Governments signed an agreement in 1895 which fixed a final boundary between the two spheres. This gave Sierra Leone its present frontier (with some slight modifications since). The line was drawn in geographical not political terms — that is, it followed lines of latitude and river watersheds, not African state boundaries. Some states were divided, part-British, part-French. As always the rulers and people were not consulted; they were merely told what had been laid down in Europe (see pages 85, 106, 110).

The British Government now had to decide how to rule its sphere. This had been discussed for some years. Many Krio wanted it annexed to the Colony and brought under English law. Parkes proposed an alternative plan — that a Protectorate be proclaimed, and the chiefs be allowed to go on ruling, with Krio District Commissioners to guide them. But the officials at the Colonial Office would not agree to Krio having authority in the Protectorate and insisted that Europeans be in charge.

Frederic Cardew became Governor in 1894. A man of considerable experience, he was, despite his age, fifty-five, physically tough. He neither smoked nor drank, and could walk many miles over rough bush paths without tiring. Within a few weeks of arrival he set out on a tour through Mende country to Panguma, then to Falaba, and back to Freetown by the Scarcies — a more extensive journey than any European had yet made in Sierra Leone.

He decided against annexing the country and trying to force English law on people who knew nothing of it. Instead he proposed a variation of Parkes's plan, a British Protectorate where chiefs still ruled — but guided by European District Commissioners. This was the sort of administration that was later introduced into Northern Nigeria by Sir Frederick Lugard under the name 'Indirect Rule'.

Cardew hoped such a government would ensure peace and open the whole Protectorate to trade, and that as trade spread the inhabitants would make money and be able to improve their standard of living.

The railway

As early as 1872 Dr Blyden suggested that a railway be built from Free-town to the interior. But nothing was done for another twenty years. By the 1890s African produce was in demand in Europe again. Trade

Fig 26 Building the railway. Top right, group with Governor Cardew in the middle; middle right, view of Freetown; at bottom, views showing railway bridges being built

recovered, and the volume of exported produce increased. All produce had to be brought on carriers' heads to the nearest riverhead and shipped to Bonthe or Freetown — a slow, laborious process. Traders proposed that a railway be built to carry it.

Cardew, anxious to increase trade, welcomed their suggestion. He went out himself, planning the route the railway should take — Freetown to Songo Town, then Rotifunk, Bo, and ultimately, he hoped, Kailahun. Work started on the first stretch, to Songo Town, in 1895, the first railway in British West Africa.

In Britain at this time railways were built and run by private companies. But the Sierra Leone Railway was built with government money and run as a government department.

The Protectorate proclaimed

The British Parliament passed an act in 1890 to enable the British Government to rule any part of the world where it claimed to have rights to rule. Such rights were claimed in the countries adjoining the Sierra Leone Colony. So on 31 August, 1896, a British Protectorate was proclaimed over all the territory on the British side of the French and Liberian frontiers.

Many people have believed that the chiefs consented to the Protectorate. They did not. Many had made treaties of friendship, but such treaties said nothing about a Protectorate. Some, in remote parts, never even made a treaty. None were asked whether they agreed to a Protectorate being proclaimed. The British Government simply declared that a Protectorate was 'best for the interests of the people'.

The Protectorate administration

Cardew introduced a simple kind of administration. The Protectorate was divided into five Districts, each under a European District Commissioner. In each District the most important rulers were given the title 'Paramount Chief'. This was a new title in Sierra Leone; until 1896 the titles 'king', 'queen' and 'chief' were normally used. But the Government wanted to emphasize that there was only one queen — Queen Victoria of Great Britain — ruling the Protectorate, and that no other person was allowed royal titles.

The Paramount Chiefs were allowed to go on judging minor cases in their own courts. In more important cases the District Commissioner sat with them. In cases that concerned slave-trading, or where war threatened, the District Commissioner judged alone.

114

The Colony's Legislative Council was given power to make laws for the Protectorate, but English law was not introduced. The Paramount Chiefs could go on using their own law. The District Commissioners were told to do what they felt was right, without being bound by any special law. Slavery was not abolished, though it was not officially recognized.

The British territory of Sierra Leone was thus divided into two distinct areas — the Colony and the Protectorate. Each was ruled separately under its own administration. This division remained until the end of British rule.

The Hut Tax

The administration was simple — only five District Commissioners in the entire Protectorate — but it brought extra expense. The District Commissioners and their clerks had to be paid. More men had to be recruited into the Frontier Police. Cardew thought the British Government should give a grant to start off the new Protectorate. But the Colonial Office stuck to its principle that colonial territories must pay for themselves (see page 85). They told him to raise the extra money locally.

Cardew did not see why the Colony should have to bear the expense of paying for the Protectorate, and decided that the Protectorate must pay for itself. Traders in the Protectorate were made to take out trading licences, but this could not raise nearly enough, so he determined on a House Tax.

He arranged that from 1 January, 1898, five shillings a year should be paid for each house. Only the three Districts nearest the Colony — Karene, Ronietta and Bandajuma — were to be taxed for the first year or two. Panguma and Koinadugu Districts, where most people were still unfamiliar with European ways, were only to be taxed when they were more used to their new government.

The traders doubted whether tax could be collected. They said the people would take to the bush rather than pay, and that trade would be ruined. The Krio anyway disliked taxes (see page 84), and said it was unfair to tax 'huts' in the Protectorate. This word 'hut' was so often used that the House Tax became known as the Hut Tax.

Reaction to the tax

Cardew went round explaining to the chiefs how they were going to be ruled. They said little. It was their tradition to be polite to governors and to agree with what they said. Most of them imagined that Cardew would soon be replaced by another governor and his plans forgotten.

When they discovered that they were under the rule of a new government, they were horrified. They did not understand why they should pay for the Protectorate administration. They had not asked for an administration and they did not want one. Nor did they understand trading licences, for they had always regarded trade as a benefit brought them by Europeans, not as something to be paid for.

Above all they did not understand the Hut Tax. They were used, as landlords, to receiving rent from their strangers. If a stranger refused them rent they would turn him out. They imagined that the Hut Tax was a kind of rent which meant that their houses were no longer theirs but belonged to the government.

They already had a bitter grievance against the British Government. Although the Frontier Police had orders to protect the people they were stationed among and not to interfere with their customs, they ignored these orders. They were posted in small detachments away from their officers, under little discipline, and could do as they liked. They would force people to work for them, rob them and take their wives. Those who complained were flogged and tortured.

The chiefs could do nothing to stop them. Frontiers tied up one Temne chief and burnt off his beard, and made another do road work. In some places the people fled into the bush at the sight of a uniform.

Now the chiefs discovered that the country was under the control of District Commissioners who would rely on the Frontiers for information. They felt they were at the Frontiers' mercy.

At Sembehun, Upper Bagru, a Temne Frontier sergeant had his friend Nancy Tucker, a woman unconnected with the country, installed as chief. At Mahera, on the Rokel, Charles Smart, a young Loko educated in Freetown, persuaded the Frontiers to get him made chief. Everywhere the chiefs saw their independence was at an end. They were losing their political power and feared the Hut Tax was going to rob them of their homes too.

Cardew stands firm

Cardew was one of the ablest governors Sierra Leone ever had. But like many capable men he preferred to go his own way without consulting others. Soon after he became Governor he had a violent dispute with Sir Samuel Lewis over an important legal case. Both were obstinate men, neither would give way, and each lost confidence in the other.

At this time several Krio officials were convicted on charges of dishonesty. This gave Cardew the impression that all Krio were dishonest. He no longer paid much attention to their opinion, nor did he seek advice from his European officials. He made decisions himself.

When the Protectorate chiefs sent in petitions of protest against the new administration, particularly the Hut Tax, Cardew was unmoved. He did not realize how strongly they felt. He believed that Krio traders were inciting them against him, and that, left to themselves, they would be quite ready to do as he wanted. He listened to their protests sympathetically but replied firmly that he was not going to change his policy and that the Hut Tax must be paid.

CHAPTER TWENTY-SIX

The Hut Tax War

Bai Bureh's War

Bai Bureh of Kasse was now aged between fifty and sixty. Since the Tambi Expedition he had had little to do with the Government in Freetown and stayed quietly at home. But he still had great influence.

Early in 1898 the District Commissioner of Karene District, Captain Sharpe, went to collect the Hut Tax at Port Loko. He began with the Krio traders. They refused to pay, explaining that the Port Loko chiefs had said they would kill them if they did. He told the chiefs they must promise not to molest the traders. They would make no promises, so he arrested five of them and sentenced them to imprisonment in Freetown gaol. The people were angry, but the arrested chiefs told them not to resist, and let themselves be taken off to Freetown.

Sharpe believed that Bai Bureh had told the Port Loko people not to pay tax. Cardew too mistrusted Bai Bureh. As there were rumours that he was preparing for war, a detachment of Frontiers was sent to arrest him.

On the way they met a large party of his men who told them to turn back. The Frontier detachment was not prepared for war. Many of them were new recruits; the officers dared not risk a fight. Back they went. Bai Bureh's men followed, dancing round them, laughing, and saying they were cowards. At last the officers could stand it no longer; they halted the Frontiers and fired, and Bai Bureh's men scattered.

This started off a war. Soldiers were sent from Freetown. The campaign was fought on the narrow bush paths in the country north-east of Port Loko. The British were armed with rifles, but most of Bai Bureh's army had only 'trade guns' with long barrels into which they stuffed old bits of iron and fired them off with gunpowder.

At first Bai Bureh's army fought in the open — but trade guns were no match for rifle-fire. Then they hid in the bush and fired at the troops marching along the narrow paths. In answer, the troops advanced firing into the bush all the way. Then Bai Bureh began building hidden stockades. His men would wait till the troops approached, then suddenly fire. The troops would halt and attack the stockade, cutting their way slowly through the bush, fired on all the time. When they reached the stockade it would be empty, the defenders having withdrawn to the next stockade further along the path. As at Tambi, they fought under strict discipline, never firing until ordered to.

The British troops belonged to the West India Regiment which garrisoned Freetown. The officers were Europeans, the men chiefly Afro-West Indians. They had little experience of bush fighting, and many fell ill. They marched with masses of equipment — food, bedding, stores — which had to be transported by carriers, so the campaign went slowly.

There were several CMS missionaries, European and Krio, in the fighting area. People in Freetown were afraid Bai Bureh would kill them, but he had no enmity towards them: he was fighting only to defend his country from invasion and left the missionaries unmolested.

Nevertheless the Rev William Humphrey, the Principal of Fourah Bay College, determined to go and look for them. The British officers told him to go home, but he paid no attention and set out towards Kasse. Two men stopped him, thinking he was a spy, and killed him. Bai Bureh was distressed at his death, and sent the missionaries safely to Freetown with a message to explain that he had had nothing to do with it.

Krio sympathy was with Bai Bureh. They disliked Cardew (who ignored their opinions), and disliked taxation, and admired a man who was ready to fight bravely against both.

Slowly the British troops moved through Kasse, destroying stockades and burning towns. Nearly a hundred towns or villages were burnt. They also attacked Bai Bureh's allies. There was a fierce struggle before they took Rowula, skilfully defended by Alimami Sattan Lahai.

Gradually Bai Bureh's resistance was broken down. When the rains began and fighting was suspended, it had almost ceased — but Bai Bureh himself was not yet captured.

The Mende War

Meanwhile in Ronietta and Bandajuma Districts the District Commissioners were collecting tax. At first there was a little opposition, but some chiefs were arrested and opposition ceased.

There were no fixed rules for collecting. The chiefs were supposed to be responsible, but sometimes Frontiers collected instead. In Shenge chiefdom the people told Thomas Neale Caulker they would not pay. He asked for help and was sent two Frontiers who went round demanding instant payment, tying up those who refused or burning their houses.

In Koya and round the Bumpe River, where people were supposed to have refused to pay, detachments of Frontiers marched about firing on any gathering of men and burning villages. By the middle of April over £2 500 had been collected from each of the two Districts.

Suddenly on 27 April the people rose. The government was taken completely by surprise. The rising had been planned secretly in a special Poro, and outsiders knew nothing about it. The many grievances about the new government, the cruel Frontiers, and the Krio traders who for many decades had lorded it over them, caused them to rise in a wave of fury against all aliens. Every European and Krio was to be destroyed, all government servants, and those who had adopted European ways — every man in trousers, it was said, every woman in a dress.

All over the Mende, Bulom and Krim countries unsuspecting traders and their families were seized and hacked to death. Some were first held prisoner and tortured. Missionaries, Krio and European, suffered with the rest. At Rotifunk six American missionaries of the UBC were brutally murdered, and two more at Taiama. Only one missionary, the Rev Charles Goodman, an English Methodist at Tikonko, was spared.

At Mafwe, near Sumbuya, the Krio gathered in the Frontier barracks to defend themselves. But their assailants poured kerosene round the barracks and burnt them out to be slaughtered. At Yele, Kittam, where there was a large gathering for the dedication of a church, they managed to escape by boat to Bonthe. The Shenge missionaries and their people got away by boat to Freetown.

The war also served as an excuse for settling personal grudges. Unpopular chiefs, particularly those friendly to the Government, were killed — Thomas Neale Caulker among them. Altogether many hundreds perished. The total number can never be known.

In Freetown people were panic-stricken. They imagined the Mende advancing into the Colony; rumours spread that they were already at Hastings. Soldiers were sent by the newly-built railway to Waterloo. But rumours and fears were groundless, for no Mende had crossed into the Colony peninsula. Gunboats were sent to protect Bonthe and save refugees congregated at the Liberian frontier.

Then two British columns went out, one from Songo Town, the other from Bonthe. But there was little serious fighting. The Mende had no Bai Bureh to lead and discipline them, and fought in disorganized bands, no match for trained soldiers. Many were armed only with clubs and cutlasses.

The first column was supported by five hundred Yoni, who sided with the British in the war. Having been once defeated by them in 1887, they were not going to risk defeat again (see page 102). They advanced through Rotifunk and took Taiama. The second column was supported by Momo Ja and Momo Kai Kai, also pro-British. There was a fierce struggle at Bumpe town, but elsewhere there was little resistance.

Panguma District was exempt from paying tax. Nevertheless, when the war broke out the Frontier officer in charge arrested Nyagua, believing he was going to take part. Nyagua's people tried to rescue him but were beaten off by the Frontiers. Then troops arrived, and Nyagua was sent to Freetown a prisoner.

By the beginning of the rains the Mende War was over. (Though it was called the 'Mende War', Vai, Loko, Temne, Bulom and Susu also took part in it.) The government decided to punish quickly those who had committed murder in cold blood, and a special judge was sent to try them. Two hundred and thirty-three were tried and one hundred and fifty-eight found guilty. Ninety-six were hanged. Large though this number was, it was far smaller than the number of those murdered.

Bai Bureh captured

The British Government thought poorly of the way the West India Regiment fought against Bai Bureh. It was decided to recruit a West African Regiment instead. In spite of the Hut Tax and the war, many Protectorate men volunteered to serve in this new British regiment. They were trained during the rains and in October took the field against Bai Bureh. Thus African soldiers under European officers opposed the famous African military leader.

There was little fighting. Bai Bureh's power was broken. But still they could not capture him. Strange stories were told of him — that he could make himself invisible or live under water.

Writing history is sometimes difficult. A historian finds two different accounts of one event and does not know which to choose. Here are two accounts of the capture of Bai Bureh.

A sergeant of the West African Regiment and some men were attacking a stockade, and the defenders fled. One ran more slowly than the rest. The sergeant fired; he threw himself down, and the sergeant seized him. It was Bai Bureh. This is the official government account. The sergeant was given a medal.

This is the other account. The soldiers were seeking Bai Bureh everywhere, but could not find him. Suddenly a tall, dignified figure emerged from the bush. It was Bai Bureh. He shouted to the soldiers not to shoot, and gave himself up with the words, 'The war done done'.

Fig 27 Bai Bureh after his capture

Bai Bureh was held a prisoner. As he had fought bravely without killing defenceless people, the Government did not want to punish him. But they dared not release him for fear he start another war, so he was deported to the Gold Coast.

He was accompanied by Nyagua of Panguma and an influential Bulom chief from Sherbro Island, Be Sherbro of Yoni. Neither Nyagua nor Be Sherbro had taken any part in the war, but the Government was afraid of them and wanted them out of the country. Both died in exile.

But Bai Bureh was allowed to return to Sierra Leone in 1905 and ended his days in his own chiefdom.

122

The Hut Tax retained

When Bai Bureh's war started, the British Government began to wonder whether the Hut Tax ought really to have been imposed, and suggested to Cardew that he reconsider it. But Cardew wanted the tax, believing it was the only way to raise enough money to pay for the Protectorate. Nor would he agree that the tax had caused the war. He said the chiefs were not really fighting against the tax, but in order to return to their old way of life, when they were free to make war on one another and capture slaves.

The Colonial Office sent a Special Commissioner, Sir David Chalmers, to investigate the causes of the war. He was also asked to consider whether the Hut Tax should go on. Chalmers was an elderly lawyer (Cardew mistrusted lawyers), and he and Cardew disliked each other at first sight. He spent several months in Freetown asking people about the war and conditions up-country. Then he wrote a report on what he had heard. He wrote that the Hut Tax was the chief cause of the war, and that it should be abolished.

Cardew answered him in another report. He repeated that the Hut Tax was necessary to raise money, and urged the Colonial Office to think of the future, to realize that the Protectorate would have to be developed one day with roads and railways which would have to be paid for. He also warned that if the tax were abolished, Bai Bureh's followers would feel they had gained a victory and that British prestige would suffer.

Cardew's arguments convinced the authorities in London and the Hut Tax was retained.

The end of the wars

The wars of 1898 are usually known by the name of 'The Hut Tax War', even though payment of tax was only one of the causes. After they had ceased, over a thousand soldiers, chiefly of the new West African Regiment, were sent marching through the Protectorate. There was no fighting. They merely showed the Protectorate peoples how strong the British Government was, how it had even enlisted their own countrymen to keep them down, and that they could have no further hope of defeating it in war.

CHAPTER TWENTY–SEVEN

The Protectorate after the war

The post-war years

Most of the Paramount Chiefs took no part in the Hut Tax War. Some, like Momo Kai Kai, fought for the Government. After it ended, their power was increased, for the Government trusted and supported them because they had been loyal.

Chiefs the Government could rely on were appointed to succeed those hanged or deposed after the war. The Rev D. F. Wilberforce became Paramount Chief of Imperi, the first Christian pastor to hold such an office. In the adjoining Banta chiefdom Bangali Margai, a member of a family the Government trusted, was chosen. Sophia Neale Caulker, an elderly lady of strong character, succeeded her cousin Thomas Neale.

Whether or not the people agreed to these changes they had to accept them. They had been defeated in war and had no alternative. As they also paid the annual Hut Tax without murmur, the Protectorate seemed to be at peace.

But some chiefs used their power to oppress their people, who dared not complain. When they collected tax they would demand more than five shillings and pocket the rest. The few District Commissioners could not control them.

The Frontier Police, back at their posts, went on illtreating those they were supposed to be protecting, getting revenge for their comrades killed in the war. People whose towns had been burnt in the war sometimes rebuilt them in remote parts of the bush, hoping the Frontiers would not find them.

So if the Protectorate was at peace, it was not ruled with law or justice.

Improved administration

Gradually the Government realized it was impossible to govern so large an area as the Protectorate with so few District Commissioners. More were appointed, they were given assistants, and the Districts were subdivided.

In 1901 the military police forces in British West Africa, including the Sierra Leone Frontier Police, were amalgamated into the West African Frontier Force (WAFF). It was a purely military body, whose members were no longer policemen but soldiers. They had to live in barracks under strict military discipline and were not allowed to wander about the country. This relieved the Protectorate of its heaviest burden — the oppressive, illdisciplined Frontiers.

Court Messengers took over the Frontiers' police duties. Originally they had been messengers, but they became a police force under the District Commissioners' orders. They did any duties the District Commissioner assigned them and he relied on them to carry on government.

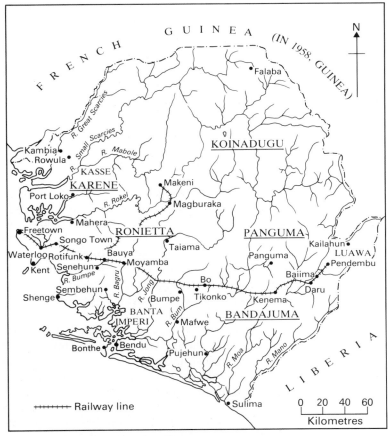

Map 5 Colony and Protectorate. The five districts created in 1896 (see page 114) are underlined

Each chiefdom was ruled by its Tribal Authority — that is, by the Paramount Chief and his sub-chiefs — but under the control of District Commissioners and Court Messengers. Chiefs convicted of oppression or misgovernment were deposed and replaced by successors the Government approved of.

The death of Madam Yoko

During the war, Senehun, Madam Yoko's town, was destroyed, but she managed to escape. Instead of rebuilding Senehun she moved to Moyamba, where the District Commissioner was building his head-quarters, and settled there under his protection. Supported by the Government, she enlarged the Kpa-Mende chiefdom until it was the biggest in the Protectorate.

Then, at the height of her power, in August 1906, she took poison and died. She felt she had achieved all she wanted — wealth, honour, position, love — and that life could offer her no more. So she preferred to die in her glory by her own hand rather than live to grow old and feeble and have to give place to others.

Fabunde's victory in Luawa

As we have seen, the frontiers of Sierra Leone were drawn without considering the frontiers of the African states that composed it (see page 112). Luawa was divided up between Sierra Leone, French Guinea and Liberia. The capital, Kailahun, was within Liberia, though the Liberians did not attempt to rule it. Luawa was no longer one country.

After Kai Lundu died his successor Fabunde was determined to bring Luawa together under one government. He chose Sierra Leone. He made friends with the British, and took no part in the Hut Tax War. He realized that the British and French were rivals, and that neither liked the Government of Liberia (because it was black). By skilful, patient diplomacy he persuaded the Government in Freetown that it was to the advantage of the British to have the frontiers redrawn, to bring the whole of Luawa within the Protectorate — though in fact it was his own advantage, the unity of his own chiefdom, that he was really concerned with. Eventually he succeeded. In 1911 and 1912 treaties were signed by which the French and the Liberians gave up their parts of Luawa. The Liberians were given part of the Gola forest, further south, in compensation.

All over Africa kings and chiefs were forced to accept the partition of their countries by European governments. Fabunde was one of the very few, perhaps the only one in all Africa, to succeed in having the frontiers changed for his own benefit.

The railway

The railway was built from Freetown through the southern part of the country. By 1908 the main line reached Pendembu, the terminus. A branch line, Bauya-Makeni, was added in 1914.

It was difficult to build. There were many rivers to be crossed, with long bridges. Bridges are expensive, and if fast trains travel over them they have to be specially strong. So, to save money, it was decided to build a railway that would only take trains going at thirty-two kilometres per hour. This was the fastest speed allowed; if they went faster, they would bring down the bridges.

Labourers flocked to build the railway. They were pleased to earn wages, which they could not get at home in their chiefdoms, and their wage, ten pence a day, seemed good money to them. So there was no shortage of labour, and few labour disputes.

At this time Europe was preparing for war, and it was discovered that palm oil could be used to manufacture explosives. Palm kernels were used to make margarine, a cheap substitute for butter. So there was a great demand for palm produce, and the volume of exports increased steadily. In 1912 over three times as much was exported as in any one year before the railway was built.

This was the main purpose of the railway — to transport produce to Freetown for export to Europe. It was not built to encourage people to travel round the country. Much of the Protectorate was remote from the railway line, and the fares were too high, and the trains too slow, for people to use it for regular travel. This was deliberate. The Government did not want people to move about, but to stay at home quietly, under the eyes of their chiefs.

Protectorate land

When the Protectorate was established the government had to consider whether people should be allowed to buy and sell land there as they could in the Colony. Some enterprising people wanted to develop it. They believed it was rich in minerals as well as vegetable produce, and.

127

hoped to start mines and plantations. But the government was afraid of development, and wanted the Protectorate to be a quiet country ruled by chiefs and District Commissioners, without outsiders coming in to make trouble. Laws were passed to make it difficult for anyone to start any industrial enterprise there. It was also declared that the land belonged to the inhabitants and that they were not allowed to sell it.

Education in the Protectorate

Christian missions returned to the Protectorate after the war and opened a few small schools. In 1904 the EUB founded the Albert Academy in Freetown where Colony and Protectorate boys could be educated together. They also opened a girls' boarding school at Moyamba (later known as the Harford School for girls) on land given by Madam Yoko.

The Government did not want the Protectorate people to have European education. Official policy was to keep the country quiet, as it was feared that if children were given education they would be dissatisfied with their chiefs and begin demanding a new government.

In 1906 a government school was opened at Bo for chiefs' sons. Here the boys were not given a European education but were trained to be satisfied with life in the Protectorate. But you cannot train people to be satisfied: once they get a little education they will want more. After about thirty years the Government was forced to realize this, and allowed Bo School to develop on the lines of other European schools.

Otherwise people went on educating their children as they always had done, at home and in the secret societies, while Muslim children went to Koranic schools run by Muslim teachers.

Divide and rule

In the 1880s and early 1890s Sierra Leone was becoming a country of large states (see page 104). Under British rule this changed. The British did not want powerful African rulers. Gradually the large units were split up. Masimera was divided after the Hut Tax War, as Bai Simera was regarded as hostile. Panguma was similarly divided after Nyagua's imprisonment. Kpa-Mende was divided after Madam Yoko's death. After Suluku died his chiefdom was split up into several small Limba chiefdoms. Even Luawa, which Fabunde had brought into Sierra Leone as one unit, was divided in two after his death. Over succeeding decades more and more small Paramount Chiefdoms were created until there were over two hundred.

The British justified these divisions on grounds of 'tribalism'. They alleged that Sierra Leone was divided among separate 'tribes' which must be kept apart. But, as we have seen, tribal feelings played little part in political life in pre-colonial days (see pages 3, 90). Indeed feelings of tribal identity and hostility were greatly increased during the period of British rule.

Similarly the Government justified its methods by saying that it was preserving 'traditional' rule. But the British system of rule was not 'traditional'. Chiefs lost many of their old powers and gained others. Chiefdoms were divided up. Chiefs were sometimes deposed, which had never happened before.

In any case many of the chiefs had not themselves been guided by tradition. Kai Lundu, Nyagua, Madam Yoko and Suluku had all supplanted the existing forms of government and created new systems of their own. They did not rule by tradition.

The chiefs ceased to be sovereign rulers, and were now under orders. Yet they also derived benefits from British rule. So long as they collaborated with the Government, the Government helped them to put down opposition or criticism within their chiefdoms. Previously they had had to respect their people's opinions. Now they could ignore them, if they chose, knowing that if there was trouble they could call on the Government for help.

So if their powers were reduced, they were given new powers to enable them to dominate their chiefdoms more easily.

CHAPTER TWENTY-EIGHT
Sickness and health

General health

In every country of the world there are many diseases. Some can be easily cured, others are often fatal. Until the twentieth century medical science had only limited success in curing disease. Most people in the world died young.

In Sierra Leone, as elsewhere, expectation of life was low. Most children never grew up. Many who grew up suffered from poor health. But, though we know that the rates of mortality and sickness were high, we cannot speak accurately about the general health of the population in the past. This is only possible when reliable health statistics are available, showing when people are born, what illnesses they have and when they die.

In Freetown people were supposed to register births and deaths, but many never bothered. Those who went to hospital had their diseases recorded, but many preferred to be treated by unqualified country doctors who kept no records. So we cannot tell for sure whether they were healthier or less healthy than people in other parts of the world at that time.

Of the Protectorate we know even less. There neither births nor deaths were registered. Country doctors who practised there could treat some diseases, but many were beyond their powers. Mortality among babies and children was particularly high. So it is likely that people there lived shorter and less healthy lives than in Freetown.

Diseases

Malaria is prevalent in Sierra Leone. It is caused by the female anopheles mosquito, which has to bite human beings in order to breed. But until the end of the nineteenth century no one knew this. People supposed it was caused by breathing in bad air. Towards the middle of the century it was realized that those who drank quinine, a bitter medicine, every

day did not get the disease, but still no one suspected the mosquito.
Inevitably many people were infected with malaria. Some died from
it, others had poor health all their lives. Europeans particularly suffered
from it, and often died soon after their arrival in the country.

There were also periodic outbreaks of another mosquito-borne
disease — yellow fever. Most people were mildly infected with it in
childhood and became immune. Europeans who caught it usually died.
So Sierra Leone was known to Europeans as 'The White Man's Grave'.
Those who lived there came only to work as officials, missionaries or
traders, intending — if they survived — to return eventually to Europe.
They did not come to settle for life.

Nor was it realized that many intestinal diseases are carried by organisms
that live and breed in water. Most people drank contaminated water
regularly and damaged their health without knowing it.

Conquering disease

Gradually medical researchers began to find ways of curing disease. By
the eighteenth century it became known that if people were inoculated
with vaccine from a cow infected with a disease similar to smallpox,
they did not get it themselves. This proved valuable in Sierra Leone.
Recaptives were often landed with smallpox caught on the slave-ships,
and vaccination prevented it spreading. Fula and Mandinka traders
were shown how to vaccinate, so that they could prevent epidemics when
they returned to their homes.

In the last decade of the nineteenth century two British doctors,
Patrick Manson and Ronald Ross, discovered that mosquitoes carry
malaria. Ross came to Freetown in 1899 and did experiments which
proved it. At last it was possible to fight malaria, by destroying the places
where mosquitoes breed. Since the 1930s drugs have been invented
which, if taken regularly, may prevent people from getting it. In the
1940s a safe and reliable immunization against yellow fever was invented.
Clean water supplies, with piped water, have been gradually introduced.
With uncontaminated water to drink, people have become healthier.

Insect and parasite invasions

Many people kept horses in Freetown in the early days. During the 1850s
they suddenly started dying off from a disease that paralysed their
hindquarters. No one knew why. People stopped keeping horses and

were carried about in hammocks instead. Traders who came by horseback from the north would leave their horses at Kambia, Great Scarcies, and go on by canoe.

When Ross was in Freetown one of his assistants discovered the cause — a tsetse fly. Tsetse flies bite horses and cattle and infect them with trypanosomiasis, a disease which paralyses and kills them. Tsetse flies must have arrived in Freetown in the 1850s — though no one then knew it. Tsetse flies do not breed in high forests, only where there is shade close to the ground. It may be that when the tall forest timber was cut down all over the coastal area and exported to Europe the tsetse flies moved in (see page 38), and that the timber trade, as well as depriving Sierra Leone of an important natural resource, also spread disease.

Jiggers, the small parasites that bore into the feet, were either rare or unknown in Sierra Leone until 1882. In that year someone imported a sheep from Liberia which was infected with them, and they spread quickly through the whole country. At first people did not know how to deal with them. Some tried to cut them out and died of blood-poisoning. But they soon learnt to extract them safely.

So insects and parasites, as well as humans, can suddenly invade a country.

CHAPTER TWENTY-NINE

The white empire

Rule by colour

As we have seen, British policy changed during the last years of the nineteenth century (see page 106). The four small coastal West African colonies were all enlarged to create a vast empire with millions of inhabitants.

This new empire was ruled on a strict principle — that white men must give orders, and that Africans must obey. This principle was new. In Sierra Leone many Africans had held senior government posts (see pages 77, 96). In 1892, of about forty senior posts, eighteen (nearly half) were held by Africans. Yet twenty years later, although, with the creation of the Protectorate, the government service had greatly expanded, and the number of senior posts had risen to ninety-two, Africans held only fifteen of them, and five of these fifteen were abolished as their holders retired.

Fig 28 Reception at Government House, 1911. The Europeans are most prominent. Some chiefs sit on the ground to the right

They were not excluded because they were inefficient but because they were African. Even the government's medical policy was based on colour. It was deliberately decided that no African doctor, no matter how well qualified, should be senior to a European doctor. Merit was unimportant. Status went by colour.

Thus British policy sought to keep authority as far as possible in the hands of white officials, and to ensure that no African should ever be in a position to give orders to a white person. This is how the empire was ruled.

Hill Station

During the nineteenth century Africans and Europeans all lived together in Freetown in a friendly way. Senior African officials or rich business men would invite Europeans to their houses, and Europeans invited them to theirs. When balls were given in the Wilberforce Hall, they all danced together.

But as the number of European officials grew and Africans lost their official seniority, the Europeans became more exclusive. Africans were invited less to their houses and were not encouraged to invite them to theirs.

After Ross had proved that malaria is carried by anopheles mosquitoes, the Government decided to move the European officials away from Freetown, where people were infected by malaria, and anopheles were plentiful, to an isolated site in the hills above, away from infection, where there were fewer anopheles. There Hill Station was built. Only Europeans were allowed to live there. A special railway line was built to take officials down to work in Freetown in the morning and bring them back in the evening. In 1929, when most officials had cars, the railway was given up.

Hill Station was built for medical reasons — to protect Europeans from malaria. But it also made it easier for them to live their own social life. Isolated in the hills, they saw little of the African population except on business. So in social life, as in government service, there was a barrier fixed between European and African.

Business competition

As the trade in palm produce increased, more European firms did business in Sierra Leone, attracted by the hope of big profits. These firms were rich. People in Europe invested money in them, and this money, the firm's capital, could be used to develop business. They could afford to employ large staffs to buy and sell. When they bought produce up-country they could buy on a large scale and give presents to chiefs. They also opened shops where they would sell at lower prices than their rivals to attract customers. Sometimes they would even sell at a loss, knowing that in the long run they would gain from the increased number of customers.

Krio business men could not compete with them. They had little capital and could not efford to make even small losses or pay large staffs of employees. When they tried to buy produce up-country they would find the firms had got in first. Many District Commissioners disliked them and wanted to keep them out of the Protectorate; it was believed that they sometimes advised chiefs to do business with European firms instead.

During the 1890s Lebanese and Syrian traders from what was then the Turkish Empire began arriving in Freetown. At first they were mostly street traders, selling coral beads (they were nicknamed 'Corals') and other small articles. Soon they were making profits and opening shops. They went into the Protectorate to buy produce and opened shops there too. They helped one another, putting their money together to buy up wholesale goods or large quantities of produce.

In the 1840s recaptives, too, had combined in this way (see page 50). But their descendants would not. They competed as fiercely against one another as against outsiders — and outsiders took their trade. European firms slowly drove them out of large-scale buying and selling, and Lebanese traders out of small-scale.

The Krio decline

Thus in the early years of the twentieth century the Krio lost what they had gained in the nineteenth. Though they had education and administrative experience, they were kept out of government posts because of their colour. After Sir Samuel Lewis died in 1903, the government paid little attention to what their members of Legislative Council said. Their hopes of achieving self-government came to nothing (see page 95).

CHAPTER THIRTY
Years of bitterness

The 1914–18 War

From 1914 until 1918 the European nations were at war — Britain, France and Russia against Germany, Austria and Turkey. Most of the nations of the world were drawn in, and their colonies had to take part. Freetown became an important British war base; the Sierra Leone Battalion of the WAFF helped to defeat the Germans in Cameroon, then a German colony. Many were also recruited to serve as carriers for British troops fighting in East Africa and the Middle East.

The rule of seniority by colour was applied in the army as elsewhere in government service. Only one Sierra Leonean, Dr M. C. F. Easmon, was commissioned as an officer.

Post-war hardships

The post-war years brought great hardships. In 1918 an epidemic of influenza spread over the world. Millions died — more, it is said, than were killed in the 1914–18 War. It reached Freetown in August and then spread inland. Whole families died. There were not enough men to farm the land and food was scarce.

Trade was depressed in Europe after the war. As always, Sierra Leone, which depended so much on import-export trade, suffered too. The Freetown naval establishment was cut down and many lost their jobs. Prices rose with the scarcity of food, but wages remained low, so in 1919 the railway workers went on strike, demanding more money.

Many people blamed the Lebanese for the country's misfortunes. They were accused of buying up all the rice, to sell it at high prices. Riots broke out against them in Freetown and then spread all over the country. Lebanese were attacked and their shops plundered. Soldiers had to be called out to restore order. Eventually they were compensated for their losses.

After the railway strike, the railwaymen founded a Railway Workers

Union, to represent their interests. Their conditions of service were poor, and in 1926 they went on strike again. But the Government refused to listen to their grievances, and forced them back to work. There was great sympathy for the railwaymen, but they were powerless against the Colonial Government.

Political demands

Educated people in the British West African colonies resented being excluded from positions of authority by their white governments. They remembered that in 1865 the British Parliament had recommended handing over power to Africans (see page 71), and demanded more say in running their countries.

In 1920 delegates met in Accra and founded the National Congress of British West Africa to press for a greater share in government. The Sierra Leone delegates were F. W. Dove, a Freetown business man, and Dr Herbert Bankole-Bright, a medical doctor.

The British Government refused to recognise the National Congress as the voice of the West African people. But, as a result of their protests, new constitutions were introduced. Sierra Leone was still governed by the 1863 constitution (see page 70). In 1924 it was revised. More African members were included in the Legislative Council, but Europeans were still in a majority.

Three of the African members were chosen by election, to represent the people of the Colony — though only those who could read and write, and owned a certain amount of property were allowed to vote. The rest were chosen by the Governor. They included three Paramount Chiefs, who were chosen to represent the Protectorate. Such small constitutional changes could not satisfy those who longed for self-government.

The members of the National Congress were wealthy men — doctors, lawyers and business men. Embittered though they were, their protests were cautious. They feared to anger the Government or stir up violence.

But in the 1930s a new leader emerged, I. T. A. Wallace-Johnson, who protested outspokenly. Born in Wilberforce village, he spent much of his life in Europe and in other parts of West Africa, attacking colonial rule. He organized his followers in the West African Youth League. In 1938 he returned to Freetown and made violent speeches which roused great enthusiasm. The Government was terrified of him. He was given a prison sentence for criminal libel, and then kept in detention for several years. In these ways the Colonial Government silenced African protests during the 1920s and 1930s.

Fig 29 Dr H. C. Bankole-Bright (1883–1958)

Fig 30 I. T. A. Wallace-Johnson (1895–1965) addressing a political meeting

CHAPTER THIRTY-ONE
Slow development in the Protectorate

Education

The prosperity of the Protectorate depended on agriculture. The Government wanted to introduce European methods of farming to increase agricultural output. But if people were to learn these new methods they needed a European type of education.

The Government therefore opened a few small primary schools in the Protectorate, and a college at Njala to train primary school teachers. However, as usual, most education was left to missionaries. The Protestant missions, associated in the United Christian Council, started their own, larger teacher-training college, Union College at Bunumbu.

But as the number of schools increased, the churches and missions could no longer afford to finance education on their own. In 1929 the Government accepted responsibility for maintaining schools. A government secondary school, the Prince of Wales School, was opened in Freetown in 1925. Though it was a Colony school, Protectorate boys could go there too. But only a tiny handful from the Protectorate reached secondary school level. The vast majority had no schooling at all, as there were not enough schools.

Slavery abolished

Slavery still continued in the Protectorate (see page 115). The Government was unwilling to abolish it, for fear of antagonising the chiefs. A few slaves served in the British forces in the 1914–18 War, and returned to their masters when it was over.

Eventually people in Britain got to hear of it and were very angry. They felt it scandalous that slavery in any form should be allowed in a British territory — particularly in Sierra Leone, where the Colony had originally been founded as a refuge for freed slaves. So in 1927 slavery was abolished. The masters made no protest. Many slaves preferred not to leave them but stayed on as servants since no other employment was available.

Mineral wealth

The rich iron ore deposits in northern Sierra Leone were worked by Africans for many centuries (see page 4). But Europeans did little to exploit the country's mineral wealth until 1926 when the Government sponsored the first geological survey. As well as iron ore, available in large quantities at Marampa, gold and chromite were discovered.

A private company, the Sierra Leone Development Company, was formed in London in 1930 to work the Marampa deposits. A railway was built to take the ore from Marampa to Pepel, where it was put into ships and exported abroad to be processed into steel.

In 1931 two large diamonds were picked up near Kenema, and an even richer diamond supply was discovered in Kono. Governments like to regulate diamond mining. They fear that if too many diamonds are mined the price will fall. So the Sierra Leone Government gave an international company, the Selection Trust, a monopoly — the sole right to mine diamonds anywhere in Sierra Leone. In return, the Selection Trust gave the Government a share of its profits. The Selection Trust headquarters was at Yengema, Kono.

Idara

In the early 1930s world trade was again depressed. The prices of agricultural produce fell so low that farmers could scarcely afford to pay their tax. There was great bitterness against the Government.

Most Muslims accepted colonial rule. But a few still wanted to bring the country under the rule of Islam, like the leaders of the *jihads* long ago (see page 14). Idara was a devout teacher who crossed over from French Guinea into Kambia District. During 1931 he went round preaching, telling the people that if they became strict Muslims God would help them, and warning those who refused that they would be killed. When the government ordered him out of the country he took up arms and told people not to pay tax.

The Government was alarmed and sent a detachment of soldiers under a white officer to arrest him. Idara's followers fired from the bush, and the officer was killed. The soldiers fired back, killing Idara and several of his followers. The rest were rounded up and imprisoned.

Though most people in Sierra Leone did not themselves dare to fight against the powerful Colonial Government and its army, they admired Idara for his courageous stand and regarded him as a hero.

The Protectorate after forty years

Plainly the Government was in no hurry to develop the Protectorate. It preferred that it should stay much as it was, under the rule of its chiefs. A few roads were built, strong enough to take motor lorries, but most of the country remained without motor transport. There was not even a motor road from Freetown into the Protectorate until 1940.

Local government was carried on by the Tribal Authorities (see page 126). The Colonial Government began to feel that the people should have more share in local affairs. From 1937 'Native Administrations' were gradually introduced. Paramount Chiefs agreed to stop collecting money directly from their people. Instead tax was paid into a chiefdom treasury. Part of the tax money went on salaries to the Paramount Chiefs and chiefdom officials. The rest was to be spent on schools, sanitation and other local services.

Forty years and more of British rule had brought little change to the Protectorate. Most people lived much the same sort of lives that they had been living before 1896. A few had been able to take advantage of the opportunities offered by European education, had received some schooling and adopted new life styles. But the majority remained in their villages, carrying on their old way of life.

CHAPTER THIRTY-TWO

The 1939–45 War and its results

The 1939–45 War

Another European War broke out in 1939, and once more the world was drawn in. Freetown again became an important base. It was far more important than it had been in the 1914–18 War because the British lost control of the Mediterranean, and all troops and supplies sent to the East had to go via West Africa. Hundreds of ships called every week. Money was poured out to build defences and large camps for the troops stationed there. Good roads were built and a small airport at Hastings, the first in the country.

Thousands of labourers were needed for these military constructions. A Labour Department was set up to organize them. They joined trade unions and learnt to combine for their own interests.

Sierra Leoneans took more part in the Second World War than in the First World War. Some served with distinction as officers in the Royal Air Force. Seventeen thousand men joined the Sierra Leone Regiment; a battalion was sent to the Far East to fight the Japanese and fought in the campaign that defeated them in Burma.

British policy changes

Britain suffered greatly from the enormous expense of the war. Some of the Far Eastern colonies were lost to the Japanese and only recovered after a hard struggle. All over the British Empire people were demanding more share in governing their countries. The Government realized that it was losing control.

It was necessary now to make a choice: either the Empire must be held down by force, or the member countries must be allowed self-government.

The first choice was impossible. Even had the British wanted to hold on to the Empire by force they were no longer strong enough. So successive British Governments agreed to adopt the second choice, and to encourage the colonial territories to become self-governing states within the Commonwealth. In this way it was hoped to avoid war or violence, and to hand over power in a peaceable way to friendly African governments.

From the middle of the war therefore the way was slowly prepared for the political independence of British West Africa. The colour bar was removed from government service. Africans were again appointed to senior posts, and given more responsibility for making and administering laws. New constitutions were prepared.

Colonial Development and Welfare Acts

The British Government had long maintained that colonies should pay for themselves (see pages 85, 115). Now it agreed that money paid by British tax-payers should be used to develop the colonies. Colonial Development and Welfare Acts were passed which authorized the expenditure of British money on colonial industries, roads, schools, and medical and welfare services.

For centuries people in Britain had profited from the colonies. Firms had made big profits by manufacturing goods to sell there, while the colonies had supplied produce at low rates and enabled the British workers to buy their food cheap. Now some of the profits were restored. But the expenditure also benefited the British economy, as most of the roads, schools and hospitals were constructed by British firms.

CHAPTER THIRTY-THREE

The road to independence

The Stevenson Constitution

In 1947 a new constitution was announced by Governor Stevenson. There were still to be Executive and Legislative Councils with white official members, but Africans were to be in the majority. The distinction between Colony and Protectorate was retained. Fourteen members of the Legislative Council would represent the Protectorate, seven the Colony.

The population of the Protectorate greatly outnumbered that of the Colony — about two million to about sixty thousand. But scarcely ten per cent of the Protectorate people could read or write. In the Colony most people were literate, indeed many had high educational qualifications. It was therefore felt that the Colony must have a large proportion of representatives, seven out of twenty-one, even though its population was so small.

But even this large proportion did not satisfy many Colony people. They wanted a majority of seats. Since 1865 they had been looking forward to the day when the British would withdraw and let them take over (see pages 71–2). Now they felt the British were betraying them, by putting them under the control of the Protectorate people. Their representatives, including Bankole-Bright and Wallace-Johnson, opposed the proposed constitution angrily. The Government was unwilling to introduce it against their protests.

While the Government delayed, a new political party was founded, the Sierra Leone People's Party (SLPP). It was led by Dr Milton Margai, the son of a rich trader in Bonthe, related to the ruling family of Banta chiefdom (see page 124). He had been educated at Albert Academy and Fourah Bay College, and had then studied medicine in England. He was the first man from the Protectorate to qualify as a doctor. His brother Albert, the first Protectorate man to qualify as a lawyer, was another member. Another was Siaka Stevens, also educated at Albert Academy, who had been General-Secretary of the Mineworkers Union at the Marampa mine.

The SLPP included some Colony people but it was predominantly a Protectorate party. It demanded that the Stevenson Constitution be introduced at once. As compromise seemed impossible, the Government introduced it in 1951. An election was then held. The SLPP gained an overwhelming victory over Dr Bankole-Bright's party, the National Council of Sierra Leone, and secured a large majority in the Legislative Council.

The members of the Executive Council were chosen by the Governor. They were his advisers, responsible to him, not ministers, responsible to the legislature and the electorate. But in 1951 the Governor chose only SLPP members of the Legislative Council to serve on the Executive Council. Dr Margai approved them first. This was the first step towards cabinet, or responsible, government — but it was only the beginning, as the Governor and four senior officials still retained their seats.

In 1953 the unofficial members of Executive Council were given the title of 'Minister' and each was made fully responsible for a government department; the following year Dr Margai became 'Chief Minister'.

Fig 31 The Governor's Executive Council, 1953. Milton Margai, who was to become first Prime Minister, stands in the front row, second from the left; his brother, Albert, who was to become second Prime Minister, stands in the middle of the second row; in the middle of the back row stands Siaka Stevens, who was to become third Prime Minister and first President

A unified police

As the Colony and Protectorate were no longer distinct political units, they did not need separate police systems. In 1954 the Court Messenger Force was abolished, and the Sierra Leone Police took over responsibility for law and order throughout the country.

Education

Now that Sierra Leone was advancing towards independence it became clear that education must be provided on a far larger scale. More schools and teacher training colleges were built. From now on, expenditure on education was a priority.

During the war the army took over the buildings of Fourah Bay College, and the students had to move out. After the war the CMS no longer had funds to re-establish it or to keep it going. It looked as if this was the end.

There was a great outcry at the threatened loss of Fourah Bay College. So in 1948 the British Government agreed to give grants to start it again on Mount Aureol above Freetown. The Sierra Leone Government undertook to support it, but it was not a government institution. An independent body, the College Council, was set up to govern it. In 1960 it became the University College of Sierra Leone.

Economic development

During the early 1950s more and more men moved from all over the country into Kono and the other diamond producing areas, to dredge diamonds from the river-beds. This was illegal. Only the Selection Trust was allowed to mine diamonds (see page 140). But when large fortunes can be made, people will defy the law, and there was a rush to mine illegally. By 1956 it was estimated that between fifty and seventy thousand people were mining.

Many who had never owned more than a few shillings suddenly became rich. They bought expensive cars and fine clothes. The Selection Trust complained to the Government, but it was difficult to prevent illegal mining over such a large area. Many people also thought it wrong that one firm should have the sole right to all the diamonds.

So the Government paid the Selection Trust one and a half million pounds. In return the Trust agreed to give up its monopoly and mine

Fig 32 Men illegally washing gravel for diamonds

Fig 33 Earth-moving equipment at the Marampa iron-ore mine

only a comparatively small area. Elsewhere mining was opened to anyone who took out a licence from the Government.

The Marampa iron ore, which was of high quality, was in great demand overseas. So the export of minerals increased steadily, and the Government received a growing annual revenue.

With more money available the country could at last be developed seriously. More roads were built, and steel bridges substituted for ferries across the rivers. The whole country was opened to motor transport, which replaced porterage and transport by boat. The old river-heads (see page 60) ceased to be important. The new developing centres were along the roads.

International trade and travel were also made easier. A new airport was laid out at Lungi, and in Freetown a deep-water quay was built so that ships could land cargo and passengers directly. Until then they had had to anchor in the harbour while everything was laboriously trans-shipped into small boats. But the railway, expensive to maintain and run, and with only slow-moving trains (see page 127), was gradually run down.

So the 1950s were prosperous years. Wealth was spread through the country. Revenue in 1950 was just over three million pounds — by 1958 it was over ten million pounds. The country was now readier to bear the financial burdens of independence

CHAPTER THIRTY-FOUR
Independence achieved

The demonstrations of 1955–56

It was not just colonial rule that people were anxious to be rid of; many of them also hated the system of local government. The changes introduced since 1937 (see page 141) still allowed chiefs to oppress their subjects. Local Councils were introduced, to give people more say in running their affairs, but they made little difference. Power still remained in the hands of the chiefs and the chiefdom officials. More and more tax was demanded, and the taxpayers felt they were getting little in return.

From 1948 onwards there were regular outbursts of angry feeling against chiefs and local government officials in different parts of the country, notably in Luawa and Pujehun. With the building of new roads, and the great migration of diamond diggers, people began to move about the country as never before, discussing their many grievances and demanding reforms. Early in 1955 there was a strike which set off violence and looting in Freetown, where the cost of living was rising and wages were still low.

Later in the year there were violent demonstrations all over the northern part of the country, from Kambia to Moyamba, against oppressive chiefs and officials. For three or four months people attacked them and destroyed their property. The Government appointed a Commission of Inquiry which found that the people's anger had been justified — that all over the disaffected areas there had been oppression and extortion.

But Dr Margai was unwilling to make any serious change. Related himself to a ruling family, he sympathized with the chiefs. In any case, he was cautious and conservative, preferring to take over the existing system from the British rather than introduce a new system.

Constitutional changes

In 1956 the Legislative Council was abolished and replaced by an elected House of Representatives. Male taxpayers were allowed to vote. Special seats were reserved for Paramount Chiefs. A general election was held in 1957 and the SLPP was returned to power. All the European officials with the exception of the Governor left the Executive Council. Dr Margai became 'Prime Minister'. In 1960 the Governor, Sir Maurice Dorman, also left, making it a cabinet, responsible to the House of Representatives.

Some of the younger cabinet ministers disliked Dr Margai's methods of government, and did not wish to go on being associated with him. Several of them, including Albert Margai and Siaka Stevens, broke away from the SLPP and formed a party of their own.

The British Government was committed to transferring political power to an independent government (see pages 142–3). Now that the SLPP was established as the dominant party, they were anxious to hand over responsibility. Sir Milton Margai (he was knighted by Queen Elizabeth II in 1959) was on the best of terms with them. So a conference was called in London to discuss arrangements for independence. Before it met, Sir Milton persuaded the opposition parties to join him in a coalition, the United National Front, to negotiate together with the British.

Arrangements were amicably agreed in London. But not all the delegates accepted the terms. Siaka Stevens had always insisted that there must be another general election before independence. This was refused. He broke away from the coalition, and in 1960 formed a new party, the All Peoples Congress, with a younger, more radical, leadership than the SLPP, presenting their policy in a militant fashion.

Sir Milton took fright. Fearing violence, or even civil war, he declared a state of emergency. When Independence Day approached, the APC leaders were arrested, and detained in prison for a month until the celebrations were all over.

CHAPTER THIRTY FIVE
The Margai Governments

Sir Milton's Government

Independence Day was 26 April 1961, the end of British colonial rule. Sierra Leone still remained in the Commonwealth, and Queen Elizabeth II was still nominally Head of State. But her authority was exercised through a Sierra Leonean Governor-General, Sir Henry Lightfoot-Boston, a distinguished lawyer. Political decisions were made henceforth in Sierra Leone, not in London.

Independent Sierra Leone was one country. The names 'Colony' and 'Protectorate' were no longer meaningful. The former Colony was renamed 'Western Area', and the former Protectorate 'the Provinces'. But one important distinction remained — the Protectorate land system (see pages 127–8), which was still retained in the Provinces.

A general election for Parliament (as the House of Representatives was now called) was held in 1962. All adult men and women had the right to vote. Once again the SLPP was successful. Sir Milton remained Prime Minister. But the APC emerged as a strong opposition party.

Favourable prospects

Prospects for independent Sierra Leone seemed favourable. Mineral resources provided revenue for development. Also, during these years, foreign money was available for the newly independent African countries, given as loans or aid, from Europe and America, and from international agencies. So the development of transportation networks and social services continued. Industries were started, to manufacture goods that had hitherto been imported from abroad.

Education was always a priority. More schools were built, and the Milton Margai Teacher Training College was founded. Fourah Bay College was enlarged, and a new university college opened at Njala. In 1969 the two colleges joined together as the University of Sierra Leone. Health services were also improved and new hospitals opened.

151

Now that Sierra Leone was independent it could take its place among the nations of the world. A foreign service was started to conduct relations with other countries. Ambassadors were sent abroad; foreign embassies came to Freetown. Sierra Leone was represented at the United Nations, and at the Organization for African Unity (OAU) founded in 1963. A new currency was introduced, leones replacing British pounds (two leones to one pound).

Sierra Leone's cultural heritage, ignored under colonial rule, was now officially cherished. A National Dance Troupe was formed. Its magnificent display won the first prize at the New York World's Fair in 1964.

Fig 34 The Sierra Leone National Dance Troupe

Sir Albert's Government

Sir Milton Margai died in April 1964. His brother Albert (knighted as Sir Albert) succeeded him as Prime Minister, and SLPP rule continued.

But the SLPP was losing its popularity. Many who had respected Sir Milton feared his brother. They believed that he would introduce constitutional changes to put down all opposition by force, and keep himself and his party in power permanently. It was suspected that the

Government was corrupt, and that politicians were enriching themselves out of public money. Agricultural production was declining, and the country seemed less prosperous. There was also the long-standing resentment against oppressive and dishonest local government.

So when an election was held in 1967, the APC votes outnumbered those for SLPP.

CHAPTER THIRTY-SIX

The Coup and return
to parliamentary rule

The 1967 Coup

In many African states army leaders seized power from civilians during the 1960s. It was the same in Sierra Leone.

When the head of the army, a Margai supporter, heard that Siaka Stevens, as leader of the APC, was being sworn in as Prime Minister, he arrested him and his supporters, hoping to keep Sir Albert in power. But the other army officers intervened. With the support of the police they took power themselves. A National Reformation Council, consisting of army and police officers, headed by Colonel A. T. Juxon-Smith, became the government of the country.

The National Reformation Council

At first the NRC was quite popular. It was hoped that it would end corruption, improve the economy and then restore power to civilians. But time passed and the officers showed no sign of giving up office. People grew disillusioned.

Among the lower ranks of the army there was also discontent. In April 1968 they arrested their officers and forced them to resign. Civilian rule was restored, and Siaka Stevens became Prime Minister.

The APC in power

Though parliamentary government was restored, and the country was ruled by a Prime Minister with long political experience, there was still discontent. People had become unsettled by the 1967 coup, and there were several further attempts to seize power by force during the next few years. They were however frustrated.

At independence Queen Elizabeth II had continued to be Head of State. But this arrangement was inconvenient. It was felt more appro-

154

Fig 35 Street scene in Freetown in the 1970s

priate to have a Sierra Leonean Head of State. So in April 1971, ten years after Independence, Sierra Leone became a Republic, still remaining within the Commonwealth.

Siaka Stevens was first Executive President and Head of State, and Sorie Ibrahim Koroma first Prime Minister and Vice-President. A general election was held two years later, and the APC was returned to power without any opposition in Parliament. Another election was held in 1977, and again the APC retained power. In June 1978, after a referendum, Sierra Leone became a one-party state.

CHAPTER THIRTY–SEVEN

The Republic of Sierra Leone

Local government reform

The local government system in the Provinces was a long-standing source of grievance. In 1972 the unpopular Local Councils were suspended. Instead the Provinces were administered through the Ministry of the Interior. Chiefs and chiefdoms councils still retained some responsibilities.

International co-operation

The international frontiers of Africa were drawn by Europeans with little consideration of African interests (see page 106). After independence Sierra Leone began to draw closer to its two nearest neighbours, Guinea and Liberia. President Stevens was supported by the Government of Guinea when he was in danger from attempted coups, and was able to borrow Guinean soldiers to help him to restore order.

Fig 36 The Mano River Bridge connecting Sierra Leone and Liberia which was opened in 1976

The Mano River Convention was signed with Liberia in 1973 to establish closer economic relations between the two countries. A bridge was built across the Mano River to make it easier to travel from Freetown to Monrovia.

Economic problems

Under colonial rule the Government had always directed the economy. After independence the governments continued to direct it, and increased their control over it steadily. During the 1960s they borrowed and spent money on a large scale, and neglected the development of agriculture. The Republican Government had the task of reviving agriculture, and of paying off the heavy debts incurred to foreign firms and governments. This task was made harder after 1973 when the world price of oil went up enormously.

Diamonds and iron ore made up most of the value of the country's exports. Since the 1950s successive governments had imposed taxes and regulations on the mining industry to keep as much as possible of the wealth derived from minerals within the country. But it proved impossible to regulate diamond mining adequately. Despite all efforts, smuggling continued on a vast scale. Millions of leones worth of diamonds were smuggled out of the country without any duty being paid.

Mineral resources cannot last forever: once the minerals have been dug out of the ground they cannot be replaced. In 1975 the Marampa mine was closed because all the available iron ore had been dug out and exported. It was also announced that the supply of diamonds could not last much longer.

Now it appeared that Sierra Leone would again have to rely on agricultural production to provide the means of foreign exchange. For though the country was politically independent, it still relied on foreign markets.

Looking to the future

A national census was taken in 1975. It showed that the population had risen since independence from just over two million to just over three million. This indicated that people were living longer and healthier lives.

A country's prosperity does not only depend on its natural resources and foreign trade. It also depends on the skill and enterprise of its inhabitants. In the past the peoples of Sierra Leone have lived their lives with courage and determination. Let it be the same in the future.

For Further Reading

Much of the history of Sierra Leone remains unwritten or unpublished. There are many peoples whose history has never been written down. There are also important works which have been presented as university dissertations but have not yet appeared in print. Until they are published the general public cannot have easy access to them.

No book has yet appeared which considers adequately the history of Sierra Leone before the sixteenth century. The best book on the period from the sixteenth to the eighteenth century is WALTER RODNEY, *A History of the Upper Guinea Coast*, OUP, 1970. There are also documents relating to this period, and to every period up to 1961, in CHRISTOPHER FYFE, *Sierra Leone Inheritance*, OUP, 1964.

The period from 1787 to 1902 is examined in detail in CHRISTOPHER FYFE, *A History of Sierra Leone*, OUP, 1962. Other important studies are ARTHUR PORTER, *Creoledom*, OUP, 1963, JOHN PETERSON, *Province of Freedom*, Faber, 1969 and LEO SPITZER, *The Creoles of Sierra Leone*, University of Wisconsin Press, 1974, and two complementary studies of the Nova Scotian settlers, JAMES S. G. WALKER, *The Black Loyalists*, Longman, 1976, and ELLEN G. WILSON, *The Loyal Blacks*, Putnam, 1976. There are several biographies of distinguished Sierra Leoneans of the period — JOHN D. HARGREAVES, *A Life of Sir Samuel Lewis*, OUP, 1958, E. A. AYANDELE, *Holy Johnson*, Frank Cass, 1970, (a biography of Bishop James Johnson), ADELEYE IJAGBEMI, *Gbanka of Yoni*, Sierra Leone University Press, 1973, CHRISTOPHER FYFE, *Africanus Horton*, OUP, 1972, also HOLLIS LYNCH, *Edward Wilmot Blyden*, OUP, 1967, for though Blyden was a Liberian he spent much of his life in Sierra Leone. A good selection of Africanus Horton's writings has been edited with introduction and notes by DAVIDSON NICOL, *Africanus Horton*, Longman, 1970. CYRIL P. FORAY, *Historical Dictionary of Sierra Leone*, Scarecrow Press, 1977, contains useful biographical information.

N. A. COX-GEORGE, *Finance and Development in West Africa — The Sierra Leone Experience*, Dobson, 1961, is a pioneer study of economic history up to 1945. A. G. HOPKINS, *Economic History of West Africa*,

Longman, 1973, also contains information on Sierra Leone. STIV JAKOBSSON, *Am I Not a Man and a Brother?* Uppsala, 1972, gives a detailed account of early mission history. RUTH FINNEGAN, *Survey of the Limba People of Sierra Leone*, HMSO, 1965, has a useful historical section. Many of the judgements expressed by these and other historians of Sierra Leone have been ably re-examined in ARTHUR ABRAHAM, *Topics in Sierra Leone History: A Counter-Colonial Interpretation*, 1977. The fullest account of Sierra Leone in the twentieth century is MARTIN KILSON, *Political Change in a West African State*, Harvard University Press, 1967. For the politics of the 1920s the relevant parts of J. AYO LANGLEY, *Pan-Africanism and Nationalism*, OUP, 1970 are recommended, and for the 1930s, S. K. B. ASANTE, *Pan-African Protest*, Longman, 1977. JOHN CARTWRIGHT, *Politics in Sierra Leone*, University of Toronto Press, 1971, gives a full coverage of the period 1947–67. THOMAS S. COX, *Civil Military Relations in Sierra Leone*, Harvard University Press, 1976, covers the period of NRC rule, JOHN CARTWRIGHT, *Political Leadership in Sierra Leone*, Croom Helm, 1978, the period of the two Margais. JOHN GRACE, *Slavery in West Africa*, Muller, 1975, contains a detailed study of slavery in the Sierra Leone Protectorate and its abolition. CHRISTOPHER CLAPHAM, *Liberia and Sierra Leone*, Cambridge University Press, 1976, is an interesting comparative study of the two countries. H. L. VAN DER LAAN, *The Lebanese Traders in Sierra Leone*, Mouton, 1975, a comprehensive account of the Lebanese community, includes a survey of the economy in the twentieth century.

There are many articles on Sierra Leone history in historical and other journals, particularly in *Sierra Leone Studies*, (old series 1918–39, new series 1953 —) and in the *Journal of the Historical Society of Sierra Leone* founded in 1977. Those who want to trace them, and other works not included this brief list, are referred to H. C. LUKE, *A Bibliography of Sierra Leone*, 1925, G.J. WILLIAMS, *A Bibliography of Sierra Leone, 1925–67*, 1970, and biographical articles by P. E. H. HAIR in *Sierra Leone Studies*, x, 1958; xiii, 1960; xxi, 1967; xxvi, 1970.

Notes for Teachers

This is only a short history of Sierra Leone. If you are using it as a school text-book you should use it as a framework to which you can add details yourself. The histories of many of the Sierra Leone peoples have never been written down, and are only known by oral tradition. Try to find out oral traditions yourself, and write them down. Encourage your students to do the same.

Let them feel that you are teaching them the history of their own country — not just some facts out of a book. Help them to realize that they will be making the history of the future.

Chapter 1

Remember that the history of Sierra Leone starts like the history of every other part of the world — people gradually learnt to control their environment, and organize themselves into communities where they could live orderly lives.

Chapter 4

Islam spread slowly in Sierra Leone. Until the twentieth century the vast majority of people still practised their own religions.

Chapter 10

You should emphasise that cutting down all the trees in an area without planting new trees is wasting a country's natural resources.

Chapter 11, 13

Note how the arrival of large numbers of recaptives altered the history of Sierra Leone by introducing a completely new element into the population.

160

Chapter 14, 15, 16

These and other chapters show how the development of trade brought political changes. Economic rivalries led to war, and to the building up of new states.

Chapters 20, 21, 22, 30, 31

As the prosperity of Sierra Leone depended (and still depends) on the export of produce overseas, it was inevitably affected by the trade depressions in Europe during the 1870s, 1880s, 1920s and 1930s.

Chapter 18

You should explain that a country cannot be fully developed unless the government has accurate statistics about the population — how many people there are, how long they are likely to live, what diseases are prevalent etc. Without information of this kind it is impossible to plan properly for the future. In the past this information was lacking. Now it has to be collected, if the country is to develop.

Remember that doctors and historians work in the same sort of way. When doctors treat patients they enquire about their patients' history — how old they are, what diseases they have had, and other historical questions.

Chapter 29–35

The events described in these chapters gradually led to independence. Remember that the period of British rule did not last very long. The first British settlement only began in 1787, the Protectorate in 1896. Independence was the normal state of the Sierra Leone peoples.

Topics

History describes how individuals and groups of people change through time. We all differ from one another because each of us has our own special history. Our lifetimes have been different: no two people have had identical experiences throughout their lives. History teaches us that everyone is unique. Time has made us different from one another.

Historians must therefore be conscious that time is passing — that today is different from yesterday, and this year from last year. None of us is the same today as we were yesterday, (we are one day nearer death, though most of us are unlikely to remember it). So historians must be concerned primarily with chronology — the study of events in their proper time sequence. If we confuse the sequence we shall misinterpret the past.

For instance — Sierra Leone in 1895, before the establishment of the Protectorate, and the fighting of the Hut Tax War, was different from Sierra Leone in 1900. To confuse these two dates, and to ascribe to 1900 an event that happened in 1895, would be to misinterpret it. It offends against chronology.

A more precise instance — many people use the title "Paramount Chief" for rulers before 1896. But (as explained on pp. 3 and 11) before 1896 they were still independent sovereigns. To give them the wrong title not only devalues their former status, it misinterprets the past.

That is why we have to indicate dates — to show that one event happened before or after another. We must not overdo dating. If we make our students learn too many dates without explaining their significance we shall only annoy them. But we can and must explain the importance of chronology, and make them see events in their proper order.

But presenting events in chronological order may make it difficult to trace the course of some particular theme or topic. We are continually led away from the theme that interests us by other events that happened at the same time.

As many teachers like to teach thematically, to choose a particular topic and illustrate it over a period of time, here are some suggestions for a thematic arrangement of the events presented chronologically in this book. Other topics can be selected by using the index.

Questions

Note — Though the questions are arranged under chapters, some refer to what has been mentioned in earlier chapters, and can be used to revise what has been studied already.

Chapter 1

1 How do hunter-gatherer peoples differ from settled, farming peoples?
2 What can the study of languages tell us about the early history of Sierra Leone?
3 How were the early states organized? What kind of economy did they have?

Chapter 2

1 How did long-distance trade develop in coastal West Africa?
2 Why did Europeans buy slaves in West Africa? Why did Africans sell slaves to Europeans?
3 How was trade between Africans and Europeans organized?

Chapter 3

1 What was the effect of the Mani invasion?
2 How successful were the early attempts to introduce Christianity?
3 What political changes took place in coastal Sierra Leone in the seventeenth and early eighteenth century?

Chapter 4

1 Why was the Holy War of Futa Jalon fought? How did it affect the coastal peoples?
2 Estimate the influence of Islam in Sierra Leone at this period.

Chapter 5

1 Explain the relationship of 'landlord' and 'stranger'.
2 How did the slave trade affect the coastal peoples during the eighteenth century?
3 How did the Caulker family become important? How did Ngombu Smart gain power?

Chapter 6

1 How did Granville Sharp influence the history of Sierra Leone?
2 What happened to the Province of Freedom?
3 What arguments were used to attack the slave trade? What arguments were used to justify it?

Chapter 7

1 What were the aims of the Sierra Leone Company? Were they successfully carried out?
2 Why did the Nova Scotian and Maroon Settlers go to Sierra Leone? What did they do there?

Chapter 8

1 Explain how differences between African and English land laws affected the relations between the Koya Temne and the Sierra Leone Company.
2 Outline the story of King Tom's War.
3 Why were the coastal Temne in difficulties during these years?

Chapter 9

1 Why did the British Government take over the Sierra Leone Colony?
2 Describe Freetown in the first decade of the nineteenth century.

Chapter 10

1 What political changes were there in the coastal country in the early nineteenth century?
2 Why was timber exported? Who benefited from the timber trade?
3 Tell the story of Dala Modu.

Chapter 11

1 Who were the recaptives? How were they settled in Sierra Leone?
2 What kind of work did the missionaries do among the recaptives? How successful were they?
3 Estimate the importance of Governor MacCarthy in Sierra Leone history.

Chapter 12

1 How was Fatima Brima Kamara elected Alikali of Port Loko?
2 Why were there wars between Loko and Temne? Tell the story of the wars and their consequences.
3 Outline the decline and recovery of the coastal Temne in the early nineteenth century.

Chapter 13

1 How did the recaptives organize themselves in their new home? How did some of them become rich?
2 Why did some recaptives choose to emigrate?
3 What happened to the Muslim recaptives?

Chapter 14

1 What vegetable products were exported at this period? What were they used for?
2 How was the produce trade organised?

Chapter 15

1 Why did the Mende people become involved in the Sherbro country?
2 How did the Sherbro economy change during the 1840s and 1850s?
3 What interest did Americans take in West Africa in the early nineteenth century?

Chapter 16

1 What effect did the introduction of steamships have on the economy?
2 In what ways did Governor Hill extend British power inland?
3 Why did the Yoni gain a reputation as warriors?

Chapter 17

1 What political changes took place in the 1860s?
2 How was the Atlantic slave trade brought to an end?

Chapter 18

1 Outline the history of education in the Sierra Leone Colony up to the end of the nineteenth century?
2 Why did the Krio people imagine that the British were going to give them self-government?

Chapter 19

1 Why did the slave trade continue within Sierra Leone after the transatlantic slave trade had ceased?
2 How did the Sherbro economy develop during the later nineteenth century?
3 How much influence did Christian missions gain outside the Sierra Leone Colony?

Chapter 20

1 Why did the British Government extend the Customs area? Why did it want economic rather than political power?
2 How did the French gain control of the Northern Rivers?
3 How did the British gain control of the Gallinas estuary?

Chapter 21

1 Outline the history of the trade wars of the early 1880s. Were they 'tribal' wars?
2 Tell the story of S. B. A. Macfoy.

Chapter 22

1 Give examples of successful professional men in nineteenth century Freetown.
2 Why was Dr Blyden important?
3 How did people become rich in nineteenth century Freetown?

Chapter 23

1 What objectives did the Yoni people have? Were their objectives achieved?
2 How were the trade wars in the Sherbro country ended?
3 Why and how did rulers gain more political power during the late nineteenth century? What new states were founded?

Chapter 24

1 How did European governments change their policies in Africa in the late nineteenth century?
2 How did the British and French divide up the Sierra Leone hinterland?
3 Describe the rise and fall of Samori.

Chapter 25

1 Why was the Sierra Leone Railway built?
2 How was the Sierra Leone Protectorate governed?
3 Why did Governor Cardew introduce a Hut Tax? How did people react to it?

Chapter 26

1 Describe the career of Bai Bureh.
2 How did the war in the south differ from the war in the north?
3 Why was the Hut Tax retained?

Chapter 27

1 What happened in the Protectorate after the end of the Hut Tax War?
2 Describe the career of Madam Yoko.
3 How did the Protectorate economy change in the early twentieth century?

Chapter 28

1 Why should historians be concerned with studying the sickness and health of peoples?
2 What diseases have been prevalent in Sierra Leone? How has the treatment of them changed?

Chapter 29

1 Explain how the British used skin colour as a means of government.
2 Why did the Krio community lose power during the early twentieth century?

Chapter 30

1 Why were there economic hardships after the 1914–18 War? How did people react to them?
2 How successful were the political movements of the 1920s and 1930s?

Chapter 31

1 To what extent was the Protectorate developed during the first forty years of British rule?
2 Illustrate how, at different periods, Sierra Leone was affected by trade depressions in Europe.
3 Tell the story of Idara.

Chapter 32

1 How did World War II affect Sierra Leone?
2 Why did British colonial policy change in the 1940s?

Chapter 33

1 How did Milton Margai gain power?
2 Outline the history of education in Sierra Leone in the twentieth century.
3 How did the economy develop during the 1950s?

Chapter 34

1 Why was the country disturbed during the 1950s?
2 Describe the constitutional developments during the fifteen years before independence.

Chapter 35

1 Why did the first years of independence seem so promising?
2 Outline the political changes from 1961–67.

Chapter 36

1 Outline the political changes from 1967–71.
2 Why did Sierra Leone become a Republic?

Chapter 37

1 Describe the changes in local government between 1937 and 1972.
2 How did the independent governments of Sierra Leone draw closer to the neighbouring states?
3 How did the Sierra Leone economy change during the 1960s and 1970s?

Time chart

Note — This is an outline time chart. It is to be used as a framework to construct more elaborate charts to which other events, inside and outside Sierra Leone, should be added.

For many thousands of years
— Hunter-gatherer peoples over the whole world

From about 3000 BC
— Peoples in West Africa begin to settle down as farmers

From about 400 BC
— Peoples in West Africa begin to mine and smelt iron to make tools and weapons

1 AD
— Start of the Christian calendar

From about 300
— With the introduction of camels, trade across the Sahara increases

622
— Start of the Muslim calendar

7th century
— Arabs invade North Africa, bringing Islam

From about 8th century
— Gold trade from West Africa across the Sahara on a large scale, carried on by Muslim traders
— Large kingdoms rise and fall in the West African interior
mid-15th century
— Portuguese ships begin sailing down the African coast, reaching

171

Sierra Leone about 1460
— Regular trade begins between coastal Africans and Europeans

early 16th century
— Beginning of the transatlantic slave trade from West Africa, which lasts until the 1860s

mid-16th century
— Mani invasion of the coastal country

early 18th century
— Muslim Holy War in Futa Jalon, starting about 1725

later 18th century
— Caulker family gains power in the Sherbro country
— Beginning of British settlement 1787

early 19th century
— British Crown takes over Sierra Leone Colony 1808
— Recaptives landed regularly in Freetown until the 1860s
— Coastal Temne under threat, then recover power
— Export trade in vegetable produce (timber, then groundnuts and palm products) begins
— Liberia founded 1821
— Mende people begin moving to the coast

mid-19th century
— The British Colony gradually extends its influence
— Mende become increasingly powerful in the Sherbro country
— Yoni try unsuccessfully to gain trading centres

late 19th century
— The governments of Europe partition Africa
— Trade wars in the Sherbro during the 1880s
— Samori creates a large state, but is eventually conquered by the French
— Some new states created in the Sierra Leone area (Kpa-Mende, Luawa, Panguma etc)
— British Protectorate over the Sierra Leone hinterland 1896
— The Hut Tax War 1898

early 20th century
— The Sierra Leone Railway, begun 1896, extends into the Protectorate
— First World War 1914–18
— Political frustration and economic hardship during the 1920s

and 30s
— Second World War (1939–45)

mid-20th century
   — The governments of Europe decolonise most of Africa
   — A new constitution for Sierra Leone 1947
   — Sierra Leone independence April 1961
   — Sierra Leone a Republic April 1971

Index